Land Rover
DEFENDER 90·110·130
Mar. 1994-1998 MY
Handbook

Part No. LRL 0087ENG

Land Rover
Lode Lane
Solihull
West Midlands, B92 8NW
England

This handbook covers petrol and diesel powered Land Rover Defender models from March 1994 up to and including 1998 model year. Covered are 2.5 and 3.5 V8 petrol engines and 2.5 and 300Tdi diesel models.

Brooklands Books Ltd., PO Box 146, Cobham,
Surrey KT11 1LG, England.
E-mail: sales@brooklands-books.com   www.brooklands-books.com

Part Number: LRL 0087ENG

Printed and bound in Great Britain by
Marston Book Services Ltd, Oxfordshire

ISBN 9781855206519   Ref: LRDF2H   10T6/2404

CONTENTS

OWNER'S HANDBOOK

This handbook covers all current versions of Land Rover Defender petrol and diesel models and, together with the Owners Information & Service Record book, provides all the information you need to derive maximum pleasure from owning and driving your new vehicle.

For convenience, the handbook is divided into sections, each dealing with a particular aspect of driving or caring for the vehicle. Sections are listed on the contents page; you will find it worthwhile to take a little time to read each one, and to get to know your Defender as soon as you possibly can. Remember, the more you understand before you drive, the greater the satisfaction when you are seated behind the steering wheel.

The specification of each vehicle will vary according to territorial requirements and also from model to model within the vehicle range. Some of the information published in this handbook, therefore, may not apply to your particular vehicle.

Section Contents	Page

Introduction

OWNER INFORMATION & SERVICE RECORD

The Owner Information & Service Record book included in your literature pack contains important vehicle identification information, details of your entitlement under the terms of the Land Rover warranty, as well as useful consumer advice and information about your AA membership.

Most important of all, however, is the section on maintenance. This outlines the servicing requirements for your vehicle and also includes the 1500 km (1,000 mile) Free Service Voucher, as well as incorporating the service record slips, which the dealer should sign and stamp to certify that routine services have been carried out at the recommended intervals.

Safety warnings are included in this handbook. These indicate either a procedure which must be followed precisely, or information that should be considered with great care in order to avoid the possibility of personal injury or serious damage to the vehicle.

WARNING LABELS ATTACHED TO THE VEHICLE

Warning labels attached to your vehicle bearing this symbol mean: DO NOT touch or adjust components until you have read the relevant instructions in the handbook.

Warning labels showing this symbol indicate that the ignition system utilises very high voltages. DO NOT touch any ignition components while the starter switch is turned on!

Your vehicle has a higher ground clearance and, therefore, a higher centre of gravity than ordinary passenger cars. This will result in different handling characteristics. Inexperienced drivers should take additional care, particularly in off-road driving situations and when performing abrupt manoeuvres on unstable surfaces.

VEHICLE IDENTIFICATION NUMBER (VIN)

If you need to communicate with a Land Rover dealer, you may be asked to quote the Vehicle Identification Number (VIN).

The VIN and recommended maximum vehicle weights (dependent on market) is stamped on a plate riveted to the top of the brake pedal box in the engine compartment (this should also match the VIN recorded in the Owner Information & Service Record book). The VIN is also stamped on the right-hand side of the chassis, forward of the spring mounting turret.

In addition, as a deterrent to car thieves and to assist the police, the VIN is also stamped on a plate visible through the left side of the windscreen.

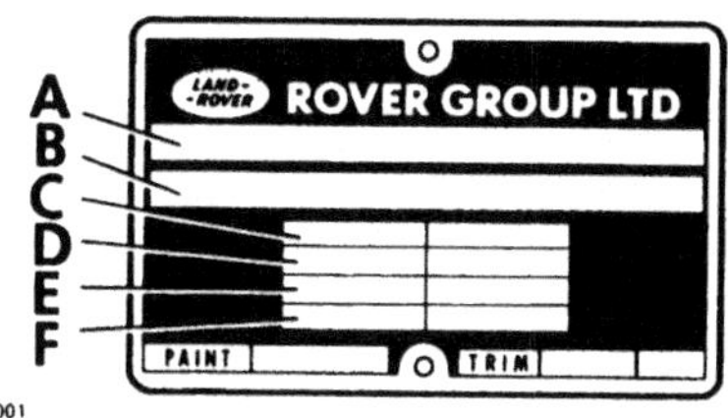

D001

A. Type approval

B. Vehicle Identification Number (VIN)

C. Gross vehicle weight (where required)

D. Gross train weight (where required)

E. Maximum front axle load (where required)

F. Maximum rear axle load (where required)

NOTE: In the interests of safety, it is essential that the gross vehicle weight, gross train weight and axle loads are NOT exceeded. For further information see 'General data'.

ANTI-THEFT PRECAUTIONS

While it may be difficult to deter the 'professional' car thief, the majority of thefts are carried out by unskilled opportunists. Therefore, take vehicle security very seriously and ALWAYS adopt this simple 'five point' drill whenever you leave your vehicle - even for just a few minutes:

- Fully close all the windows (and the sunroof).

- Remove your valuable belongings (or hide them out of sight).

- Remove the starter key.

- Engage the steering lock (by slightly turning the wheel until it locks).

- Lock all the doors.

Thieves are attracted to 'vulnerable' vehicles. Even if you have followed the 'five point' drill, there is still much you can do to make your vehicle a less inviting target.

BE SAFE NOT SORRY!

- Park where your vehicle can easily be seen by householders and passers-by.

- At night, park in well lit areas and avoid deserted or dimly lit side streets.

- At home, if you have a garage, use it - and NEVER leave the keys in the vehicle.

- Do not keep important vehicle documents (or spare keys) in the vehicle - these are a real bonus for the thief.

IMPORTANT INFORMATION

**Remember the breakdown
safety code**

If a breakdown occurs while travelling:-

- Wherever possible, consistent with road safety and traffic conditions, the vehicle should be moved off the main thoroughfare, preferably into a lay-by. If a breakdown occurs on a motorway, pull well over to the inside of the hard shoulder.

- Switch on hazard lights.

- If possible, position a warning triangle or a flashing amber light at an appropriate distance from the vehicle to warn other traffic of the breakdown (note the legal requirements of some countries).

- Consider evacuating passengers through nearside doors onto the verge as a precaution in case your Defender is struck by another vehicle.

In this section of the handbook you will find descriptions of the controls and instruments on your vehicle.

For your own safety, it is most important to read this section fully and to gain a thorough understanding of all the controls before driving.

Controls

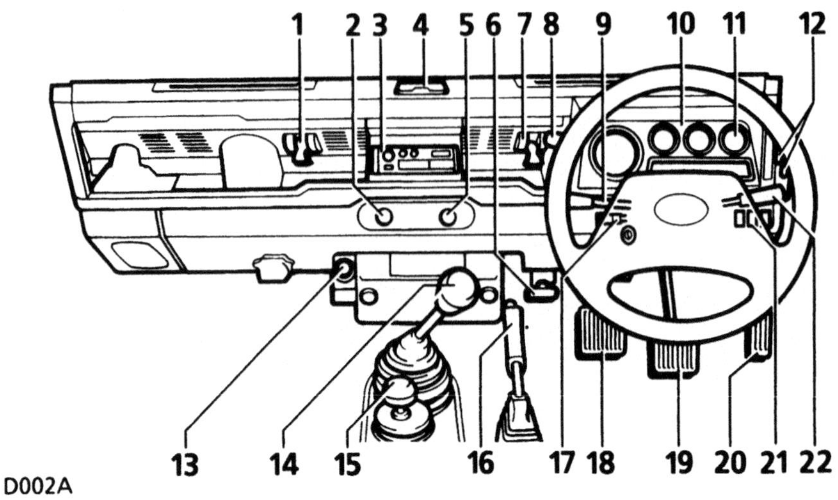

Right hand steering

1. Ventilator control

2. Rear screen wash/wipe switch

3. Radio/cassette player

4. Ashtray

5. Cigar lighter

6. Bonnet release handle

7. Ventilator control

8. Heater fan control

9. Lighting, direction indicators and horn control

10. Instrument and warning light pack

11. Clock

12. Heater controls

13. Hand throttle - if fitted

14. Main gear lever

15. Transfer gear lever

16. Handbrake

17. Main lighting switch

18. Clutch pedal

19. Brake pedal

20. Accelerator pedal

21. Rear fog guard lights, heated rear window and hazard warning light switches

22. Windscreen wash/wipe control

NOTE: *The precise specification and location of controls may vary according to territorial requirements and from model to model within the vehicle ranges.*

Controls

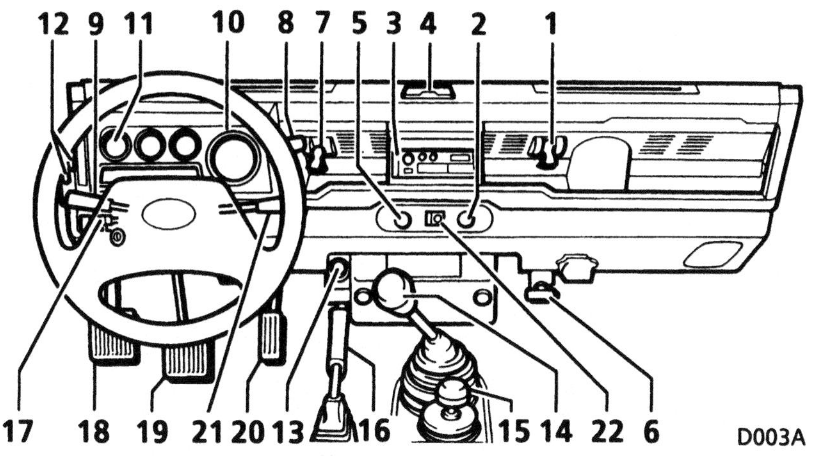

Left hand steering

1. Ventilator control

2. Rear screen wash/wipe switch

3. Radio/cassette player

4. Ashtray

5. Cigar lighter

6. Bonnet release handle

7. Ventilator control

8. Heater fan control

9. Lighting, direction indicators and horn control

10. Instrument and warning light pack

11. Clock

12. Heater controls

13. Hand throttle - if fitted

14. Main gear lever

15. Transfer gear lever

16. Handbrake

17. Main lighting switch

18. Clutch pedal

19. Brake pedal

20. Accelerator pedal

21. Windscreen wash/wipe control

22. Headlight levelling switch - if fitted

NOTE: *The precise specification and location of controls may vary according to territorial requirements and from model to model within the vehicle ranges.*

Locks & Alarm

D004A

KEYS

You have been supplied with two sets of keys, comprising:

- a black key for operating the starter switch.

- a plain, metal, key for operating the door locks and fuel filler cap.

Key numbers

The starter key number is stamped on a tag attached to the key ring. Both key numbers should be entered on the Security Information card.

For safety, remove the Security Information card from the literature pack and keep it with the key tag, and spare keys in a safe place - AWAY FROM THE VEHICLE!

Front door locks

From outside the vehicle, the door locks can ONLY be operated with the key. Turn the key towards the rear to lock and towards the front to unlock.

Door sill locking buttons

From inside the vehicle, each door can be individually locked by depressing the appropriate sill locking button.

DO NOT depress the sill buttons as a means of locking the doors from outside the vehicle (this practice - known as 'slam locking' - is NOT recommended, because keys can be locked inside accidentally).

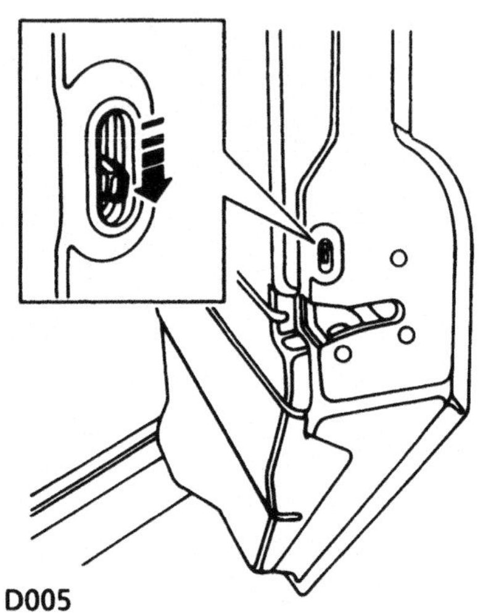

D005

Child-proof locks
(110 Station wagon)

Move the locking levers down to engage the child-proof locks (see illustration).

With the locks engaged, the rear doors cannot be opened from inside the vehicle, thereby reducing the risk of a door being opened accidentally while the vehicle is moving.

Locks & Alarm

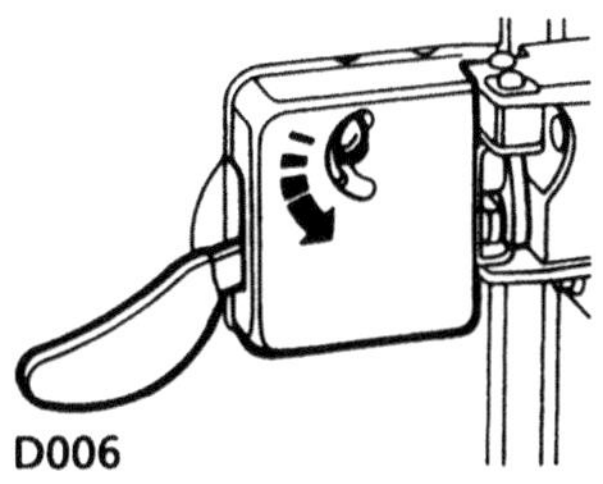

D006

Taildoor (if fitted)

From outside, use the door key to lock and unlock the taildoor. From inside and with the door closed, push the locking button up to lock and down to unlock (as illustration).

ALARM SYSTEM

Your vehicle is fitted with a sophisticated anti-theft alarm and engine immobilisation system. In order to combine maximum vehicle security with minimum inconvenience, you are advised to gain a full understanding of the alarm system by thoroughly reading this section of the handbook.

Features of the alarm system

Perimeter protection: This part of the alarm system protects the doors, bonnet and taildoor against unauthorised entry - the alarm sounding if any one of these apertures is opened without the alarm first being disarmed.

Interior protection: Also known as volumetric protection, this part of the system protects the space inside the vehicle. If movement within the passenger compartment, or intrusions through the windows or sunroof are detected, the alarm will sound.

Engine Immobilisation: The engine is immobilised electronically whenever the alarm system is armed. Even if the alarm has not been armed, engine immobilisation will occur automatically thirty seconds after the driver's door is opened, or five minutes after the starter switch is turned to position '0'.

In practice, this means it is virtually impossible to leave your Defender unattended without the engine being immobilised.

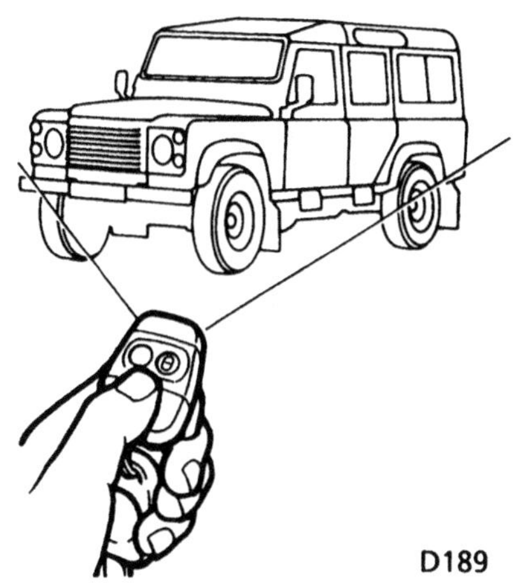

D189

ARMING THE ALARM

If a passenger or animal is to be left inside the vehicle, or if a window or sunroof is to be left open, interior protection must be disabled. Refer to 'Interior protection' before arming the alarm.

To arm the alarm, aim the handset at the Defender and press the right hand button (PADLOCK SYMBOL). Provided all the doors and other apertures are closed, the direction indicator lights will flash three times to confirm that the alarm is armed. All the security features described previously will be active.

Once armed, the alarm will sound if a door or the bonnet is opened, or if movement is detected inside the vehicle.

Disarming the alarm

Within range of the vehicle, briefly press the left (PLAIN) button on the handset; the direction indicator lights will flash once to indicate that the alarm has been disarmed and the engine re-mobilised.

NOTE: In some territories, the interior lights will illuminate when the alarm is disarmed.

If the direction indicators fail to flash when the alarm is armed:

This indicates that a door or the bonnet is not fully closed, in which case the alarm will still be partially armed and the engine immobilised, but interior protection will not be active.

Once the open door or bonnet is closed, the direction indicators will flash three times and the alarm will fully arm as described previously.

If the alarm sounds:

The vehicle horn and alarm siren will sound continuously for 30 seconds and then switch off. The horn and siren can be triggered up to three times.

To silence the alarm, press either handset button. If the handset is inoperative, the alarm can only be disarmed by entering the emergency key access code (see 'Engine immobilisation override').

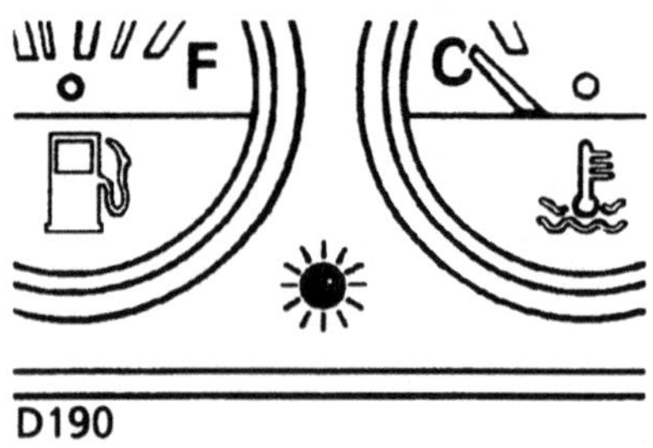

D190

Anti-theft alarm indicator light

A RED indicator light on the instrument panel indicates the status of the alarm system. When the alarm is armed successfully, the light FLASHES rapidly. After 10 seconds, the light adjusts to a slower frequency, and continues flashing as an anti-theft deterrent until the alarm is disarmed.

If the light fails to illuminate during the rapid flash phase, this indicates a 'mislock' (door or bonnet not fully closed or key in starter switch). If this occurs, the indicator light will still flash at the slower frequency as an anti-theft deterrent.

If the light illuminates continuously, this indicates that the engine has immobilised passively (see 'Engine immobilisation').

J664

Interior protection

Interior protection is activated automatically when the alarm system is armed; twin sensors inside the vehicle monitor the interior space and will activate the alarm if an intrusion is detected.

However, if passengers or animals are to be left inside the vehicle, or if a window or sunroof is to be left open, the alarm must be armed with interior protection DISABLED as follows:

To disable interior protection:
1. Open the driver's door.
2. With the driver's door open, use the handset to arm the alarm in the normal way.
3. Close the driver's door (the direction indicator lights flash three times and the anti-theft indicator light commences flashing rapidly). The alarm system is now armed with interior protection disabled.

WARNING

If the vehicle is to be left with windows or sunroof open, or with passengers or animals inside, the interior protection MUST BE DISABLED, as described above.

NOTE: *Interior protection will not operate for the first 15 seconds after the alarm is set.*

ENGINE IMMOBILISATION

Engine immobilisation is an important aspect of the vehicle's security system, and occurs automatically whenever the alarm system is armed.

The system also includes a feature known as 'passive immobilisation', which is designed to safeguard the vehicle from theft should the driver forget to lock the doors or arm the alarm.

Passive immobilisation occurs automatically:

* thirty seconds after the starter switch has been turned off AND the driver's door opened.

* five minutes after the starter switch is turned off or the alarm system is disarmed.

IMPORTANT INFORMATION

The engine immobilisation system relies on the handset to re-mobilise the engine. Look after the handsets at all times, protecting them from loss, damage and battery discharge.

If the engine has immobilised passively, re-mobilisation will occur when the starter switch is turned to position 'II', provided the handset is on the same ring as the key and in close proximity to the switch.

* ALWAYS keep the handset on the same ring as the key.

* NEVER attach both handsets to the SAME key ring.

Any attempt to start the engine while it is immobilised will cause the engine immobilisation warning light (on the left of the warning light panel) to flash.

Engine immobilisation override

If the handset is lost or fails to operate, engine immobilisation can be overridden by using the starter key to enter the four digit emergency key access code (this code is recorded on the Security Information card). The procedure for entering the code is described below.

Before entering the code, note the following:

If your handset is lost or inoperative, it is impossible to disarm the alarm. As soon as the door is opened, the alarm will sound (continuously for up to three 30 second periods), and continue while the code is being entered.

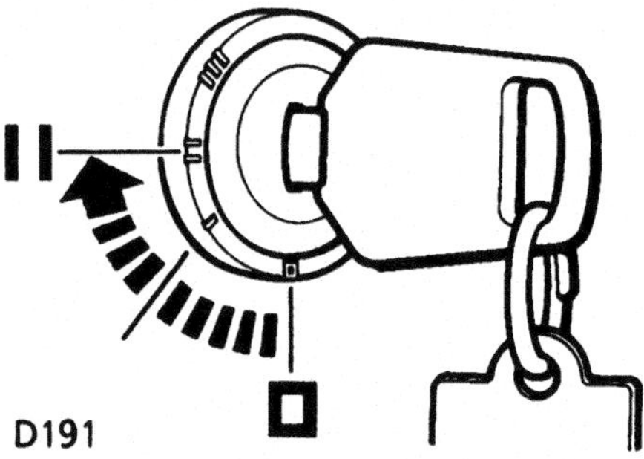

D191

1. With the driver's door closed, insert the key into the starter switch, turn to position 'II' and hold in this position for 5 seconds. Then switch off.

2. Turn the switch to position 'II' the required number of times to enter the first digit of the code (if the first digit is 4, turn the key to position 'II' and then back to '0' four times).

3. Open the driver's door (to enter the first digit) and then close the door again.

4. Turn the starter switch to position 'II' and back to '0' the required number of times to enter the SECOND digit of the code.

5. Open the driver's door (to enter the second digit) and then close the door again.

6. Turn the starter switch to position 'II' and back to '0' the required number of times to enter the THIRD digit of the code.

7. Open the driver's door (to enter the third digit) and then close the door again.

8. Turn the starter switch to position 'II' and back to '0' the required number of times to enter the FOURTH digit of the code.

9. Finally, OPEN and CLOSE the driver's door. If the code has been entered correctly, the anti-theft indicator light will extinguish and the engine can be started.

If an incorrect code has been entered:

If the code is entered incorrectly, the anti-theft indicator light will continue to illuminate and the engine will fail to start. Before entering the code again, turn the starter switch to position 'II' and hold in this position for 5 seconds.

After three failed attempts, the security system invokes a delay period of thirty minutes during which the system will not accept any further codes.

WARNING

- *NEVER leave the Security Information card in the vehicle.*

- *Memorise the emergency key access code or keep the Security Information card on your person in case of emergencies.*

Locks & Alarm

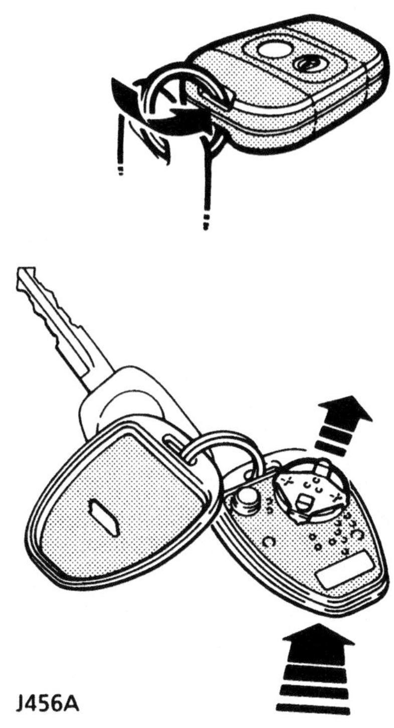

J456A

HANDSET BATTERY

IMPORTANT INFORMATION

- BEFORE replacing a handset battery, disarm the alarm and unlock the doors.

- DO NOT remove an expired battery until you are ready to install the replacement.

- The engine will immobilise five minutes after the key is removed from the starter switch. If handset battery replacement is NOT completed within this period, the emergency key access code will have to be entered before the handset can be synchronised.

The handset battery should last for approximately three years dependent upon use. When the battery needs replacing it will be apparent from the following symptoms:

- The handset will only work every other operation while disarming.

- The direction indicator lights will not flash when the alarm is disarmed.

Always fit a Panasonic CR2032 replacement battery (available from a Land Rover dealer) and adopt the following replacement procedure:

1) Unlock the vehicle and disarm the alarm system.

2) Turn the starter switch to position 'II', then turn to position '0' and remove the key.

3) Carefully prise the handset apart, start from the keyring end using a coin or small screwdriver. Avoid damaging the seal between the two halves of the case and DO NOT allow dirt or moisture to get inside the handset.

4) Slide the battery out of its clip, taking care to avoid touching the circuit board or the contact surfaces of the clip.

5) Press and hold one of the buttons for at least five seconds (this will drain any residual power from the handset).

6) Fit the new battery, ensuring that correct polarity is maintained (positive ('+') side facing up). Finger marks will adversely affect battery life; if possible, avoid touching the flat surfaces of the battery and wipe them clean before fitting.

7) Reassemble the two halves of the handset, then operate the PADLOCK symbol button at least four times within range of the vehicle to resynchronise the handset.

The handset is now ready for use.

WARNING

The handset contains delicate electronic circuits and must be protected from impact and water damage, high temperatures and humidity, direct sunlight and the effects of solvents, waxes and abrasive cleaners.

IMPORTANT INFORMATION

Battery disconnection

Your vehicle is equipped with a battery backed-up sounder, which operates as an anti-theft siren if the vehicle battery is disconnected.

Before disconnecting the vehicle battery, it is ESSENTIAL to refer to *'Battery removal and replacement'* in Section 4, in order to prevent the alarm from sounding.

If the vehicle battery is disconnected for any reason, the status of the security system prior to disconnection will be memorised and automatically reset when the battery is reconnected.

ALARM OR HANDSET DIFFICULTIES

Alarm goes off unexpectedly.	(a) Ensure all windows and sunroof are closed. (b) Disable interior space protection.
Alarm goes off when door opened.	Disarm the alarm with the handset before unlocking. If the handset has failed, enter the emergency key access code (refer to *'Engine immobilisation override'*).
Starter will not operate.	Ensure handset is on same ring as starter key. If it still will not operate, consult a Land Rover dealer.
Direction indicator lights don't flash when alarm is armed.	A door or bonnet is partially open.

FRONT SEAT ADJUSTMENT

WARNING

To avoid the risk of loss of control and personal injury, never adjust the driver's seat or seatback while the vehicle is in motion.

Forward/backward movement

Lift the bar at the front of the seat base to slide the seat forward or back. Ensure the seat is locked in position before driving.

Backrest movement

Lift the lever and lean backwards or forwards to achieve the desired angle, then lower the lever to lock.

WARNING

DO NOT allow front seat occupants to travel with the seat backs reclined steeply rearwards. Optimum benefit is obtained from the seat belt with the seat back angle set to 25 degrees from the upright (vertical) position.

D008

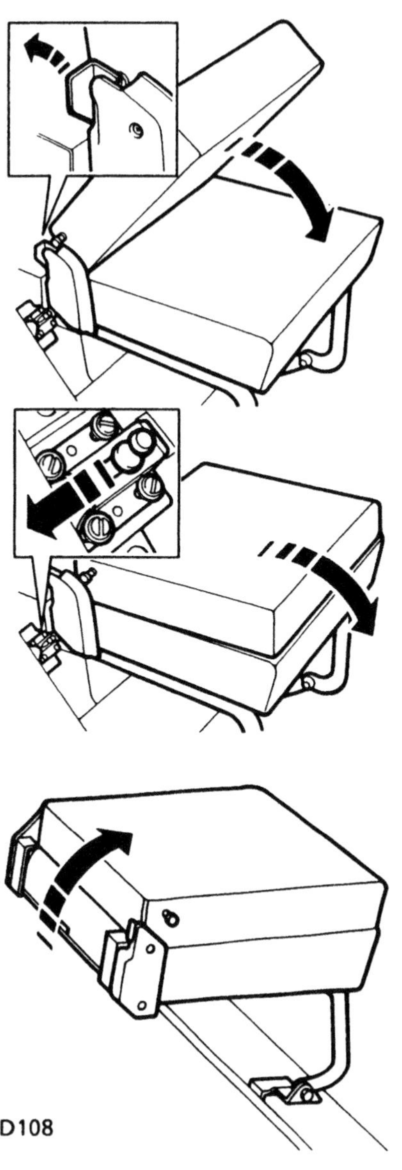

D108

FOLDING THE REAR SEATS - (if fitted)

Before folding the rear seats;

- Slide the front seats forward.

- Ensure that the outer rear seat belts are correctly stowed in their belt clips.

- Pass the seat belt locks through the junction of the backrest and the cushion and into the loadspace.

Individually split rear seats

NOTE: *The two outer seats must be folded first, thereby releasing the centre seat.*

Outer seats;

1. Release the catch (see first inset).

2. Fold the backrest forward.

3. Slide back the bolt (see second inset).

4. Lift and fold the seat base forwards.

Centre seat;

5. Release the catch - as (1).

6. Fold the backrest forward.

7. Lift and fold the seat base forwards.

When returning the backrest to the upright position, ensure it is securely latched in place before driving.

WARNING

DO NOT adjust the seats while the vehicle is in motion.

When the seat is erected, the latching mechanism should be visually checked and physically tested to ensure that the latch is secure before driving.

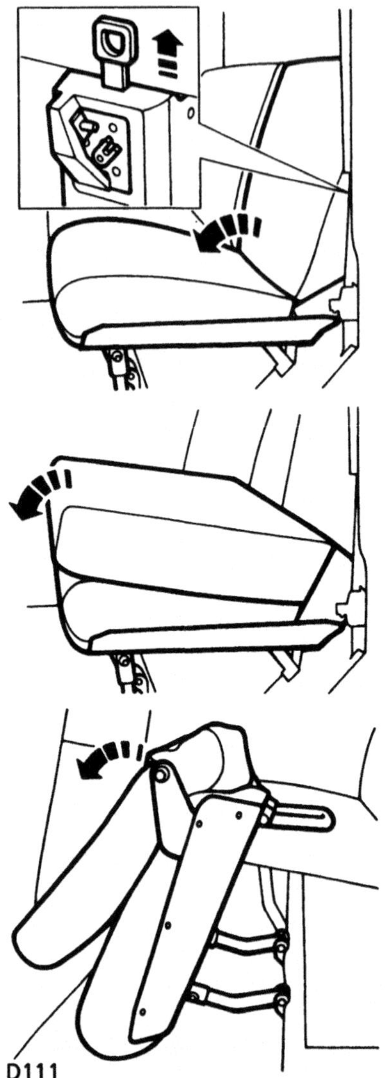

60/40 split rear seats

1. Pull up the release catch.

2. Fold the backrest forward.

3. Lift and fold the seat base forward.

4. Fold away the seat stand.

WARNING

DO NOT adjust the seats while the vehicle is in motion.

When re-erecting the seats, ensure that the seat stands are properly positioned.

When the seat is erected, the latching mechanism should be visually checked and physically tested to ensure that the latch is secure before driving.

D111

SEAT BELT SAFETY
Seat belts are life saving equipment.
In a collision, unrestrained passengers can be thrown around inside the vehicle, or possibly thrown out of the vehicle, resulting in injury to themselves and to other occupants. DO NOT take chances with safety!

- DO make sure ALL passengers are securely strapped in at all times - even for the shortest journeys.

- ALWAYS adjust seat belts to eliminate any slack in the webbing, and to ensure that the diagonal belt passes across the shoulder without slipping off or pressing on the neck.

- ALWAYS fit the lap strap as low on the hips as possible (never across the abdomen).

- DO have seat belts checked if the vehicle has been involved in an accident.

- DO NOT allow front seat occupants to travel with the seat backs reclined steeply rearwards. Optimum benefit is obtained from the seat belt with the seat back angle set to 25 degrees from the upright (vertical) position.

- DO NOT fit more than one person into a belt, or fit a seat belt that is twisted or obstructed in any way that could impede its smooth operation.

- DO NOT allow foreign matter (particularly sugary food and drink particles) to enter the seat belt locks - such substances can render the locks inoperative.

WARNING

Pregnant women should ask a doctor for advice about the safest way to wear seat belts.

D010

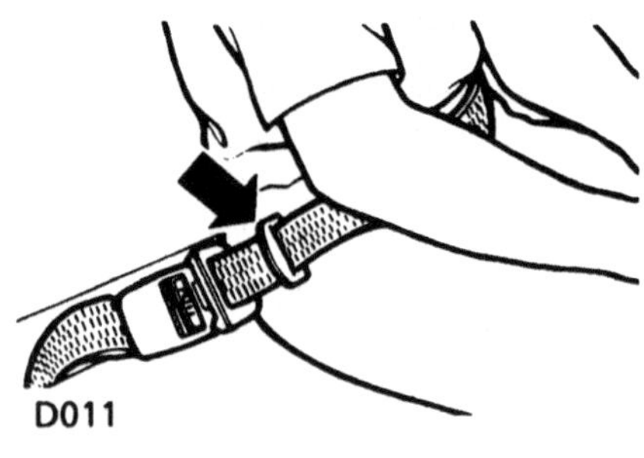

D011

At all times, occupants should wear a seat belt for their protection in the event of a collision or sudden stop. In some circumstances, perhaps due to the vehicle being on a slope, the automatic locking mechanism may engage, preventing the initial extension of the belt. This is not a fault - ease the belt free and use it.

Fastening the inertia reel belts

Draw the belt over the shoulder and across the chest, and insert the metal tongue plate into the lock nearest the wearer - a 'click' indicates that the belt is securely locked.

Seat belts are designed to bear upon the bony structure of the body (pelvis, chest and shoulders) and can only be worn safely with the webbing crossing the shoulder MIDWAY BETWEEN THE NECK AND THE EDGE OF THE SHOULDER and with the seats in a normal UPRIGHT position - DO NOT allow the front passenger to travel with the seat steeply reclined.

Lap belts

To adjust, pull the slider along the belt and feed the webbing through the buckle until the belt is comfortably tight. When not in use, the lap belts should be fastened.

Seat belts

Infant and child restraints

All infant and child restraint systems are designed to be secured in vehicle seats by means of a lap belt or the lap portion of a lap/shoulder belt.

When installing and using any infant or child restraint system, always follow the instructions provided by the manufacturer concerning installation and use. Failure to properly secure the child restraint system in the vehicle can endanger the child in a collision or sudden stop and cause injury to other passengers.

Centre and inward facing seats are fitted with lap belts which can be manually tightened to secure an infant or child restraint system. Older children should use the lap/shoulder belt fitted to the outer rear seating positions.

Never leave a child unattended in your vehicle.

Caring for seat belts

Regularly inspect the belt webbing for signs of wear, paying particular attention to the fixing points and adjusters. Always replace a seat belt that has withstood the strain of an impact or shows signs of fraying.

DO NOT bleach or dye the webbing. Clean the webbing using warm water and non-detergent soap only - allow to dry naturally and DO NOT retract the belt until completely dry.

Testing inertia reel belts

From time to time carry out the following tests:

1. With the seat belt fastened, give the webbing near the buckle a quick upward pull. The buckle must remain securely locked.

2. With the seat belt unfastened, unreel the webbing to the limit of its travel. Check that unreeling is free from snatches and snags.

3. With the webbing half unreeled, hold the tongue plate and give it a quick forward pull. The safety mechanism must lock automatically and prevent any further unreeling.

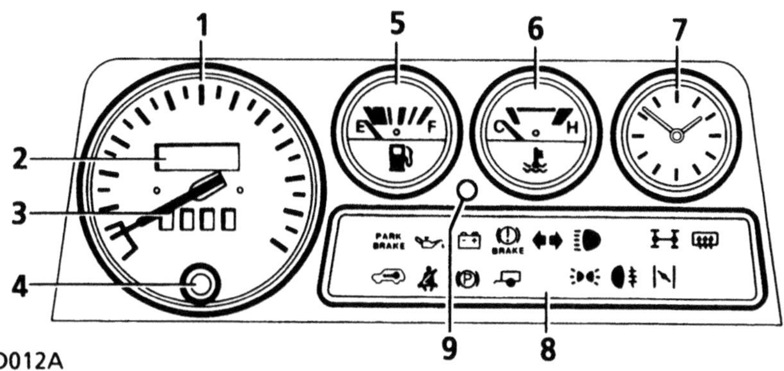

D012A

1. Speedometer
Indicates road speed in miles and/or kilometres per hour.

2. Total distance recorder
Indicates the total distance travelled by the vehicle.

3. Trip recorder
Records individual journey distances.

4. Trip recorder reset button
Press to return trip recorder to zero.

5. Fuel gauge
The pointer indicates the fuel level when the starter switch is turned to position 'II'.

6. Temperature gauge
Once the engine coolant has reached its normal operating temperature, the pointer should remain between the **'C'** (cold) and **'H'** (hot) segments. If the pointer enters the 'H' segment, stop the vehicle as soon as safety permits and seek qualified assistance before continuing.

7. Clock
To adjust the time, depress and rotate the button in the centre of the clock face.

NOTE: *The clock will need to be reset if the battery has been disconnected.*

8. Warning lights
The specification of the warning lights will vary according to model and market requirements.

9. Anti-theft alarm indicator light
Indicates the status of the alarm system (see 'Locks & alarm').

Warning lights

The warning lights are colour coded as follows:

RED lights are warnings.

DO NOT drive if a RED warning light remains on once the engine is running or illuminates whilst driving.

GREEN & BLUE lights indicate that a unit is operating.

AMBER lights show that a unit is operating and should be switched off (or rectified) as soon as conditions allow.

 **Low engine oil pressure** - RED Illuminates as a bulb check when the starter switch is turned to position 'II' and extinguishes when the engine is running. If it remains on, or illuminates whilst driving, STOP THE VEHICLE as soon as safety permits and seek qualified assistance before continuing. Always check oil levels when this light illuminates.

NOTE: At very low ambient temperatures, the light may take several seconds to extinguish.

 **Battery charging** - RED Illuminates as a bulb check when the starter switch is turned to position 'II' and extinguishes when the engine is running. If it remains on, or illuminates whilst driving, a fault is indicated. Seek qualified assistance urgently.

 **Brake system check** - RED Illuminates as a bulb check when the starter switch is turned to position 'II' and extinguishes when the engine is running and the handbrake is released. If it remains on, or illuminates whilst driving, a fault with the braking system is indicated. STOP THE VEHICLE as soon as safety permits and seek qualified assistance before continuing.

DO NOT drive the vehicle while the brake warning light is illuminated.

 **Direction indicators** - GREEN Flashes in conjunction with the direction indicators. If the light does not illuminate, this may indicate a bulb failure in the warning light pack or in one of the direction indicator lights.

 **Headlight main beam** - BLUE Illuminates whenever the main beam headlights are on.

Differential lock - AMBER
Illuminates whenever the differential lock is engaged.

If the light remains on after the differential lock is disengaged, transmission 'wind up' may be present. Reversing for a short distance and then going forward will usually 'unwind' the transmission. If the light remains on, contact your dealer as soon as possible.

Heated rear screen - AMBER
Illuminates when the rear screen heater is operating.

Engine immobilisation - RED
Flashes during any attempt to start the engine when the engine is immobilised.

Trailer direction indicators - GREEN
Flashes in conjunction with the vehicle direction indicator lights to show that all trailer indicator lights are functioning correctly. In the event of a bulb failure on the trailer, the warning light flashes once and then remains off.

NOTE: *When a trailer is not fitted, the warning light will only flash once.*

Sidelights - GREEN
Illuminates whenever the sidelights are on.

Rear fog guard lights - AMBER
Illuminates whenever the rear fog guard lights are on.

REMEMBER: In clear conditions, rear fog guard lights can dazzle other road users. Use ONLY when visibility is severely restricted.

Cold start - AMBER
Petrol engines:
Illuminates when the cold start control is operating. DO NOT operate the cold start control longer than necessary.

Diesel engines:
Illuminates whenever the starter switch is turned to position 'II' if the engine is cold. WAIT for the light to extinguish before starting the engine.

Handbrake - RED (if fitted)
In some markets, the light illuminates when the starter switch is turned to position 'II' and the handbrake is applied. The light should extinguish when the handbrake is fully released.If the light remains on or illuminates while driving, seek qualified assistance before continuing.

Seat belt warning - RED (if fitted)
In some markets, if the driver's seat is occupied, the light illuminates when the starter switch is turned to position 'II'. The light extinguishes as soon as the driver's seat belt is fastened. ALWAYS fasten your seat belt BEFORE driving!

Lights & indicators

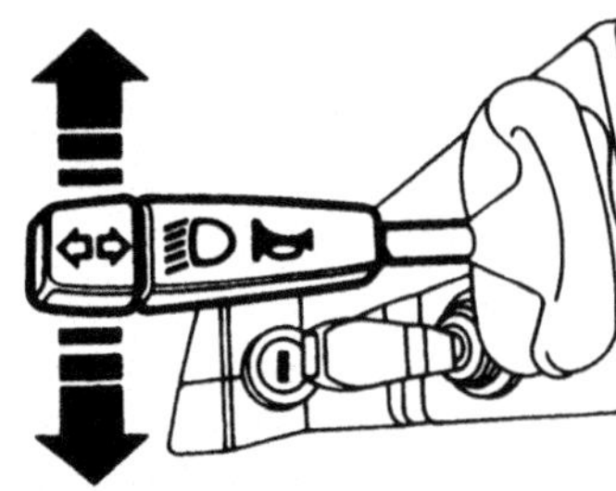

D028

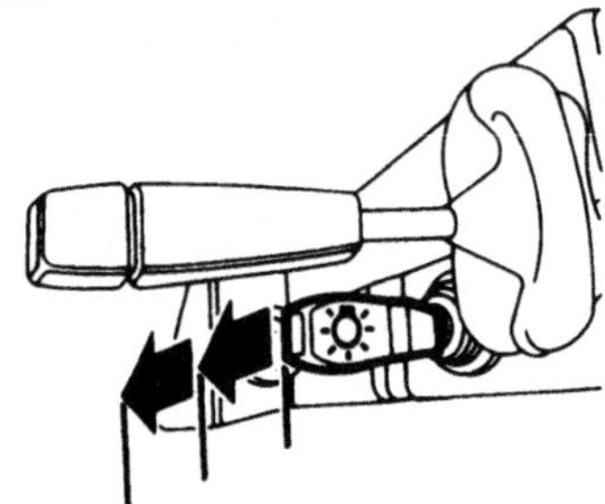

D029

D030

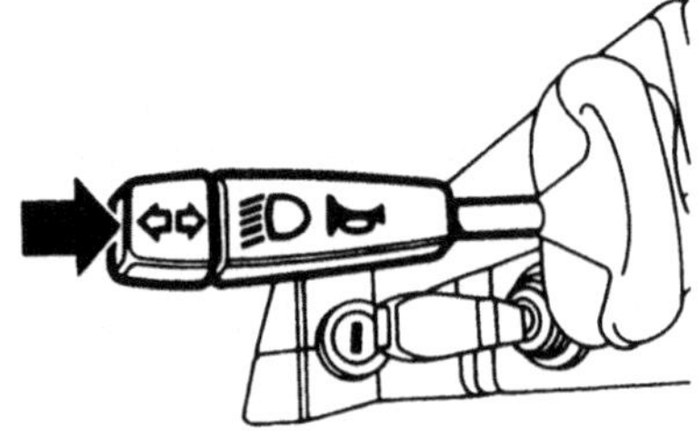

D031

Direction indicators

Move the lever DOWN to indicate a LEFT turn, and UP to indicate a RIGHT turn (the GREEN warning light on the instrument panel will flash in time with the direction indicators). Hold the lever part-way up or down against spring pressure to indicate a lane change.

Main light switch

Lever position;

- Static - all lights off

- First position - side, tail and instrument panel lights on (see 'Dim-dip' headlights)

- Second position - headlights on

Headlight main beam and 'flash'

With the headlights switched on, push the lever away from the steering wheel to activate main beam (BLUE warning light illuminates).

To flash the headlights, pull the lever part-way towards the steering wheel and then release.

'Dim-dip' headlights (UK only)
Dim-dip headlights illuminate automatically when the sidelights and starter switch are turned on. They are brighter than normal sidelights, but are of insufficient intensity to meet the requirements of UK legislation governing the use of headlights when driving in darkness or in seriously reduced visibility. In poor lighting conditions, full headlights must always be used!

Horn

Press end of the lever to operate the horn.

WINDSCREEN WIPERS

- **Single wipe**
  Push the lever up against spring pressure and release immediately.

NOTE: *With the lever held up, the wipers will continue operating at high speed until it is released.*

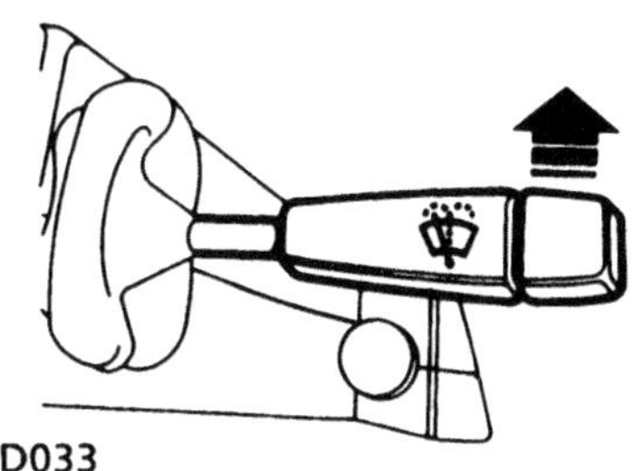

D033

- **Intermittent wipe**
  Pull lever down.
- **Normal speed wipe**
  Push lever up to first position.
- **Fast speed wipe**
  Push lever up to second position.

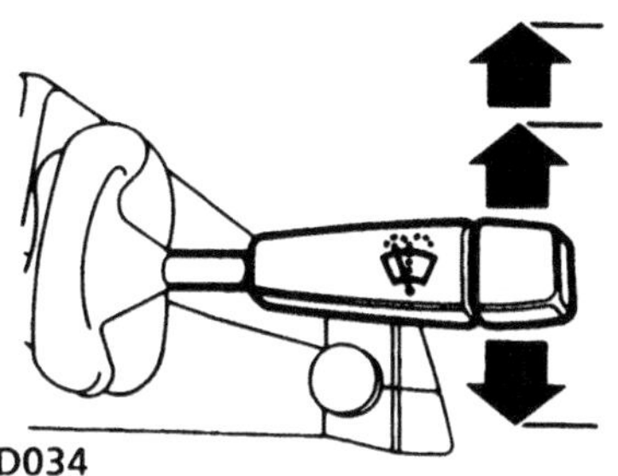

D034

- **Windscreen washer**
  Press to operate (the wipers will also operate).

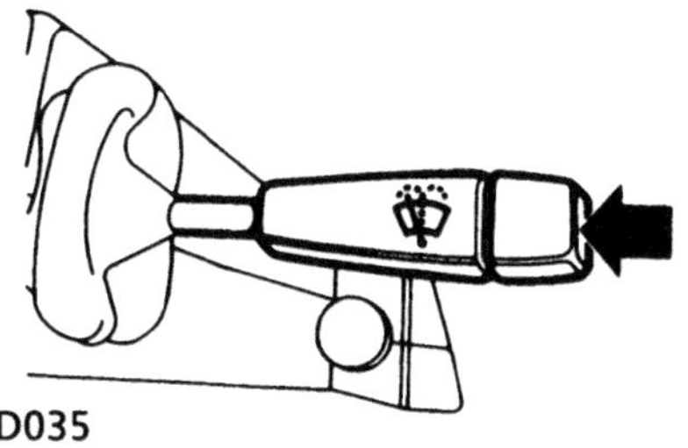

D035

D036A

Rear window wash/wipe

The rear window wash/wipe only operates
with the starter switch turned to position 'II'.

- Press and hold to operate the washer.

- Rotate clockwise and hold to operate the
  wiper for the required duration.

IMPORTANT INFORMATION

- DO NOT operate the wipers on a dry
  screen.

- In freezing or very hot conditions,
  ensure that the blades are not frozen
  or stuck to the glass.

- In winter, remove any snow or ice
  from around the arms and blades,
  including the wiped area of the
  windscreen and the heater air
  intakes.

*NOTE: If the wiper blades have stuck to
the glass, a thermal cut-out may
temporarily prevent the wiper motor from
operating. If this is the case, switch the
wipers off, free them from the
obstruction and then switch on again.*

D037

Heated rear window (if fitted)

Press the lower portion of the switch to operate; press the upper portion to switch off. The switch indicator illuminates while the heating elements are switched on and extinguishes when they are turned off.

NOTE: If the electrical system is being overloaded a cut-out switch will deactivate the rear window heater until such time that the alternator can maintain sufficient charge.

WARNING

DO NOT stick labels over the heating elements, and DO NOT scrape or use abrasive materials to clean the inside of the rear window.

Hazard warning lights

Press the lower portion of the switch to operate (switch indicator illuminates); all the direction indicator lights (including those fitted to a trailer) will flash in conjunction with each other.

Use ONLY in an emergency to warn other road users when your stationary vehicle is causing an obstruction, or is in a hazardous situation. Switch off by pressing the upper portion before moving away.

Rear fog guard lights (if fitted)

Press the lower portion of the switch to operate (indicator light illuminates); press the upper portion to switch off. The lights operate ONLY with the headlights switched on, and extinguish when the headlights are switched off. However, DO remember to switch the fog guard lights off as soon as visibility is clear - whilst the switch remains on, the fog guard lights will illuminate automatically whenever the headlights are turned on.

REMEMBER: In clear conditions, rear fog guard lights can dazzle other road users. Use only when visibility is severely restricted.

Fuel tank changeover switch
(if fitted)

On vehicles fitted with an additional (optional) fuel tank, the fuel supply can be switched between tanks as follows;

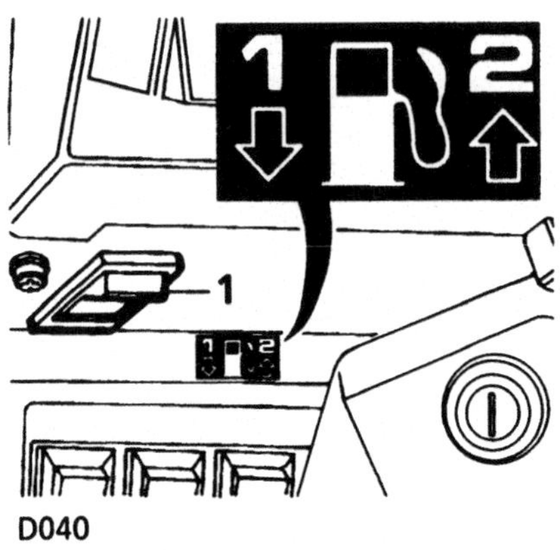

D040

D041

Petrol engines:

The switch (1) is located under the dashboard below the instrument panel. Press the lower portion of the switch to select Tank 1 and the upper portion to select Tank 2.

Diesel engines:

The combined changeover tap and switch is located on the heelboard. Pull the lever up to the vertical position to select the Main fuel tank and push the lever down to the horizontal position to select the Side tank.

NOTE: *The fuel gauge on the instrument panel will indicate the fuel level of the selected tank.*

WINDOWS

Front/rear windows;

Raise or lower the window by rotating the
handle mounted on the door trim pad.

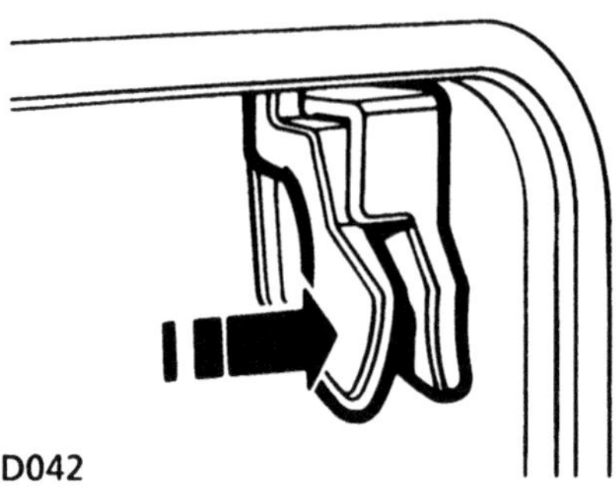

D042

Sliding rear windows; (if fitted)

To open, press the catch tongues together,
slide the window to the desired position and
release the catch, ensuring that it locates
securely in the sockets, locking the window in
position.

Sunroof

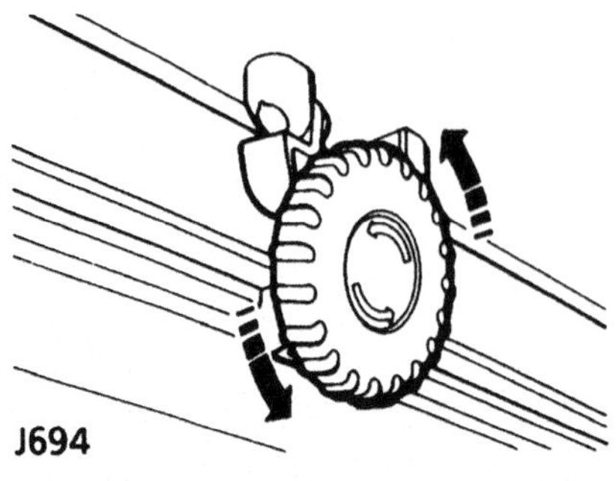
J694

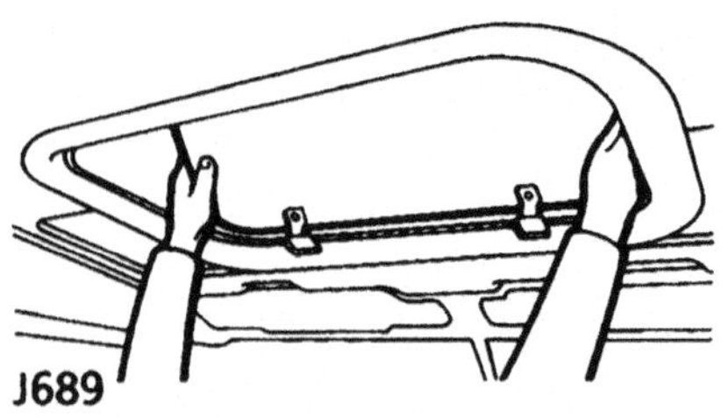
J689

Remove the sunroof by tilting upwards and lifting rearwards to disengage the locating lugs.

SUNROOF (if fitted)

The sunroof can be opened to varying degrees or, if required, can be removed completely.

To OPEN the roof:

Turn the hand wheel anti-clockwise to give the desired opening.

To CLOSE the roof:

Turn the hand wheel clockwise until resistance is felt.

To REMOVE the roof:

DO NOT store the sunroof loose in the vehicle.

DO NOT allow passengers to extend any part of their bodies through the sunroof while the vehicle is moving.

DO NOT remove the sunroof whilst the vehicle is moving.

Refit the sunroof by following the same procedure in reverse.

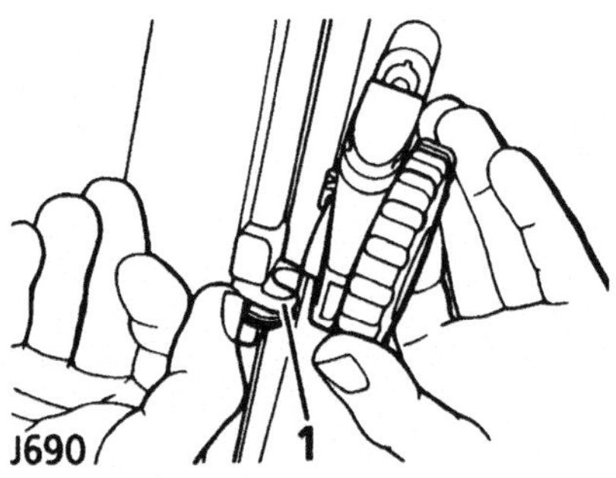
J690

Open the sunroof fully and push the catch (1) rearwards to disengage the hand wheel mechanism.

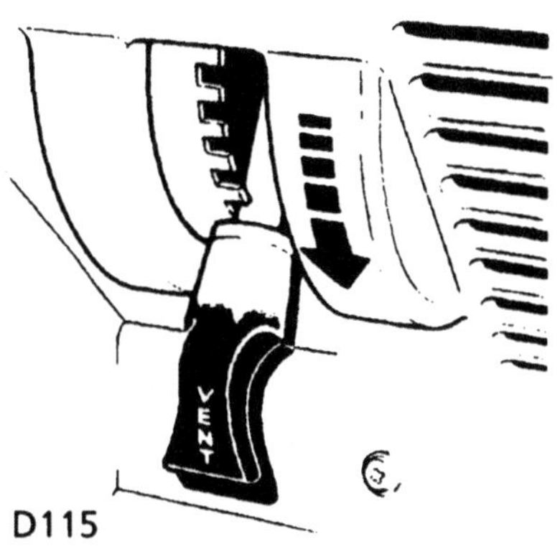

Fresh air vents

To open the two vents in the windscreen frame, push the lever to the right and then downwards to the desired position and release.

The temperature of air supplied to the fresh air vents is not controlled by the heater.

NOTE: *For vehicles fitted with an air conditioning system, the location and operation of air vents is described on a later page (see 'Air conditioning').*

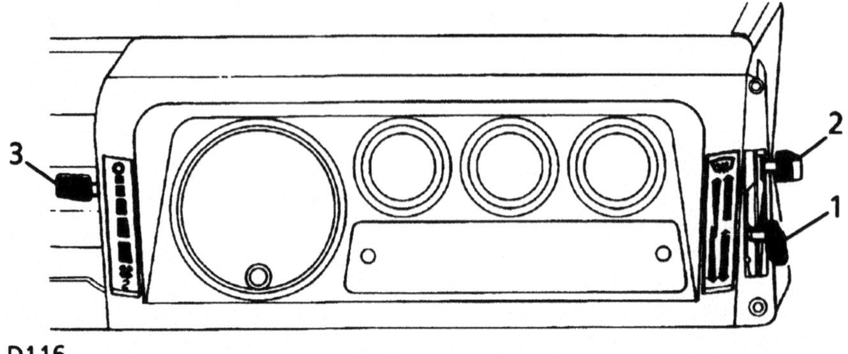

D116

HEATER CONTROLS

NOTE: For vehicles fitted with an air conditioning system, the heater controls are described on a later page (see 'Air conditioning').

1. Temperature control
Move the lever downwards (towards the RED segment) to increase air temperature, or upwards (towards the BLUE segment) to reduce air temperature.

2. Air distribution control

- Lever fully up - windscreen vents only.

- Lever midway - foot level and windscreen vents.

- Lever fully down - foot level vents (also provides some air to the windscreen).

3. Fan speed control
Move the control downwards to progressively increase fan speed. With the control at '0' the fan is stationary and the volume of air entering the passenger compartment is solely dependent upon the ram effect of the vehicle moving through the air.

USING YOUR HEATER

Ensure the front grille and the air intake grille on the front wing are kept clear of obstructions (especially snow and ice).

The following examples of basic heater settings are intended as a general guide; the air distribution, temperature and blower controls can then be further adjusted to suit your comfort requirements.

Always remember that full heating is not available until the engine has reached its normal operating temperature.

Maximum heating

- Temperature control - fully down.
- Distribution control - midway.
- Fan speed control - fully down.
- Fresh air vents - fully closed.

Demisting and defrosting

- Temperature control - fully down.
- Distribution control - fully up.
- Fan speed control - fully down.
- Fresh air vents - fully open for demisting (closed for defrosting).
- Opening a window may improve ventilation.

Maximum ventilation

- Temperature control - fully up.
- Distribution control - fully down.
- Fan speed control - fully down.
- Fresh air vents - fully open.

Air conditioning

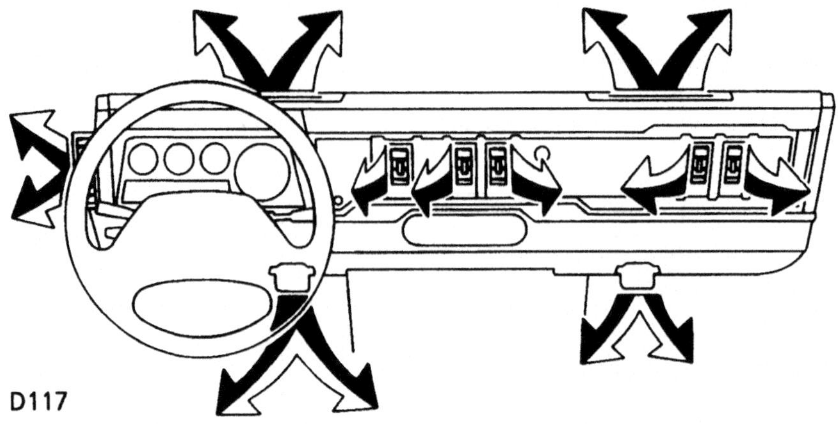

Location of air vents - (LH steering illustrated)

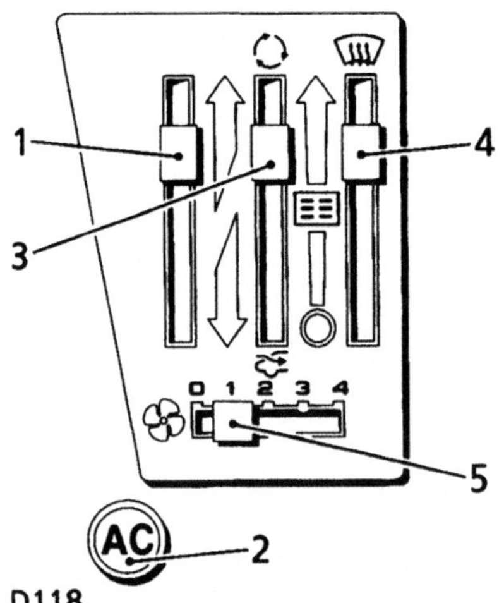

D118

AIR CONDITIONING
(if fitted) - LH steering

CONTROLS

1. Temperature control
Move the lever upwards (RED) to increase air temperature, or downwards (BLUE) to reduce air temperature.

2. Air conditioning switch
Press the switch (indicator light illuminates) to activate the air conditioning. Press again to switch off.

3. Air recirculation control
Move the lever fully upwards to activate air recirculation. Move the lever fully downwards to cancel recirculation.

NOTE: *Prolonged recirculation may cause the windows to mist up.*

4. Air distribution control

- Lever fully up - air to windscreen vents (also provides some air to the footwell).

- Lever midway - air to fascia vents (also provides some air to the footwell).

- Lever fully down - air to footwell vents (also provides some air to the windscreen).

5. Fan speed control
Move the lever to the right to progressively increase the fan speed.

Air conditioning

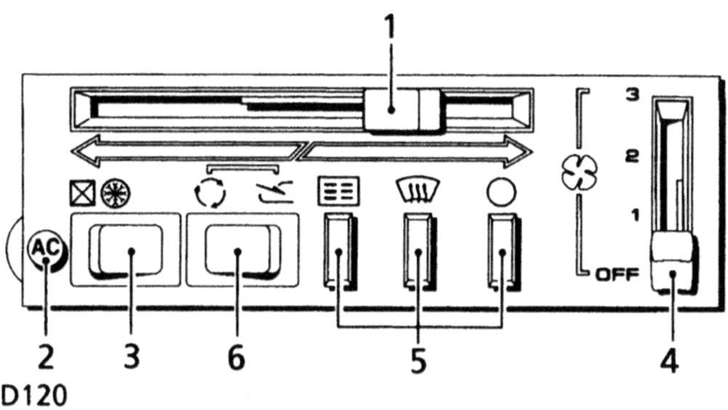

D120

Air conditioning (if fitted) - RH steering

CONTROLS

1. Temperature control
Move the lever to the right (RED) to increase air temperature, or to the left (BLUE) to reduce air temperature.

2. Air conditioning indicator light
Illuminates when the air conditioning system is operating.

3. Air conditioning switch
Press the right hand portion of the switch to activate the air conditioning (indicator light illuminates). Press the left hand portion to switch off.

NOTE: *Air conditioning should only be activated when the engine is running.*

4. Fan speed control
Move the lever upwards to progressively increase the fan speed.

5. Air distribution controls

- Push left hand button for air to fascia vents (also provides some air to footwell).

- Push middle button for air to windscreen vents (also provides some air to footwell).

- Push right hand button for air to footwell vents (also provides some air to windscreen).

6. Air recirculation switch
Press the left hand portion of the switch to activate air recirculation. Press the right hand portion for fresh air.

NOTE: *Prolonged recirculation may cause the windows to mist up.*

Air conditioning

USING THE AIR CONDITIONING

Air conditioning provides additional cooling to the vehicle interior and also reduces the moisture content of the air.

The air conditioning system will only operate with the fan switched on and the engine running. It is also important to keep the windows (and sunroof) closed during operation.

Operation of the air conditioning system, places an additional load on the engine which, in very hot conditions and if the engine is required to work unusually hard, could result in high engine temperatures. If the temperature gauge pointer reaches the RED zone, turn the air conditioning off until engine temperature returns to normal.

Air recirculation

The air recirculation mode prevents the heating system from taking in fresh air from outside the vehicle. Instead, the air already inside the vehicle is recirculated, thus preventing the entry of traffic fumes. In cold weather, air recirculation also enables warmer air to be used to defrost the windscreen when the engine is still cold.

WARNING

The air recirculation mode can cause the windscreen to mist up. If this happens, switch off air recirculation immediately.

Points to remember:

- If the temperature inside the vehicle is higher than that outside when you start the engine, it will take time for the air conditioning to become fully effective. It is best to ventilate the vehicle by opening the windows and operating the fan for a brief period before switching on the air conditioning. Remember to close the windows whenever the air conditioning is operating.

- Operating the air conditioning takes power from the engine and consequently increases fuel consumption.

- All air conditioning systems need to be operated for a short while every week (even in winter) to maintain them in peak condition.

- The air conditioning system will also dehumidify air. The surplus water produced by this process is expelled from the system via drain tubes beneath the vehicle. This may result in a small pool of water forming on the road when the vehicle is stationary and is not a cause for concern.

Air conditioning

The following examples of heater and air conditioning settings are included for your guidance:

Maximum heating

- Air conditioning switch - OFF.
- Temperature control - set to RED position.
- Distribution control - set to footwell position.
- Fan speed control - set to maximum speed.
- Air recirculation control - set to recirculation.

Demisting and defrosting

- Air conditioning switch - ON.
- Temperature control - set to RED position.
- Distribution control - set to windscreen position.
- Fan speed control - set to maximum speed.
- Air recirculation control - set to fresh air.

Maximum ventilation

- Air conditioning switch - OFF.
- Temperature control - set to BLUE position.
- Distribution control - set to footwell position.
- Fan speed control - set to maximum speed.
- Air recirculation control - set to fresh air.

Normal cooling

- Air conditioning switch - ON.
- Temperature control - set to BLUE position.
- Distribution control - set to fascia position.
- Fan speed control - set to desired speed.
- Air recirculation control - set to fresh air.

Maximum cooling

- Air conditioning switch - ON.
- Temperature control - set to BLUE position.
- Distribution control - set to fascia position.
- Fan speed control - set to maximum speed.
- Air recirculation control - set to recirculation.

Switch off air recirculation when desired temperature is reached.

Reducing humidity

These settings are suitable for normal driving.

- Air conditioning switch - ON.
- Temperature control - set to midway.
- Distribution control - set to windscreen position.
- Fan speed control - set to midway.
- Air recirculation control - set to fresh air.

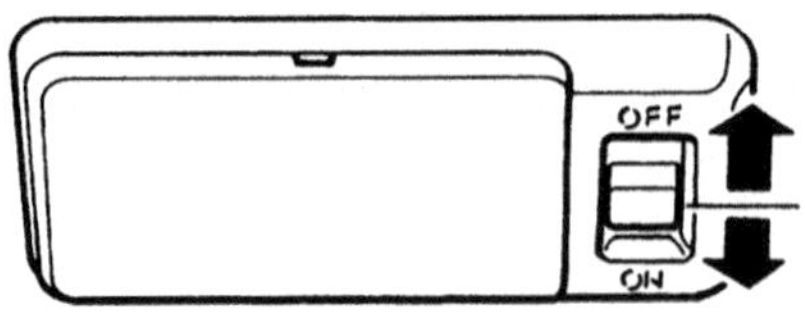

D043

INTERIOR LIGHTS

With the switch midway between the 'ON' and 'OFF' positions, the light will illuminate automatically whenever a door is opened and remain illuminated for approximately 15 seconds after ALL the doors are closed, or until the starter switch is turned on.
When alighting from the vehicle, the interior lights will fade and then extinguish as soon as the last door is closed.

NOTE: *Any subsequent opening and shutting of doors prior to the starter switch being turned on again, will cause the 15 second delay feature to operate.*

NOTE: *If a door remains open for eight minutes, a 'time-out' function will extinguish the lights to avoid discharging the battery.*

D044

CIGAR LIGHTER

With the starter switch turned to position II, press the lighter in to heat up. When it has reached the correct temperature it will partially eject and can then be withdrawn for use.

- ONLY hold the cigar lighter by the handle.

- DO NOT use the ashtray for disposing of waste paper or other combustible materials.

- DO NOT plug accessories into the cigar lighter socket unless they are approved by Land Rover.

D046

ASHTRAY

Lift the lid of the ashtray to open. To remove, carefully prise the ashtray out of the fascia panel.

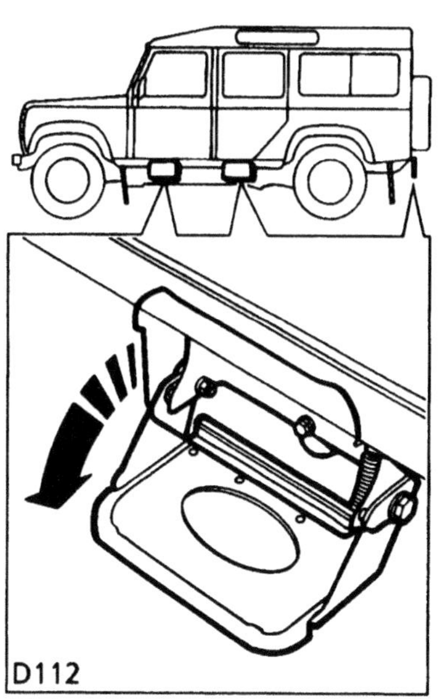

Steps (if fitted)
The steps can be folded up or down as required.

SECTION 3
Driving & operating

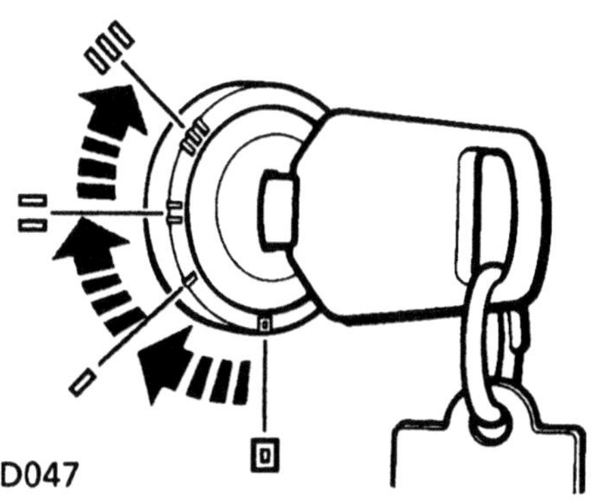

D047

To unlock the steering column
Insert the ignition key FULLY and turn the starter switch to position 'I', while turning the steering wheel slightly to disengage the lock.

To lock the steering column
Turn the starter switch to position '0' and withdraw the key from the starter switch. Turn the steering wheel towards the straight ahead position until the lock engages.

WARNING

DO NOT remove the key or turn the starter switch to position '0' while the vehicle is in motion. Once the steering lock is engaged, it is impossible to steer the vehicle.

STARTER SWITCH

The starter switch is located to the left of the steering column, and uses the following sequence of key positions to operate the steering lock, electrical circuits and starter motor.

Position '0'

Steering locked (if key is removed).

Most lighting circuits are operational, including: sidelights, headlights, hazard warning lights and rear fog guard lights.

Position 'I'

Steering unlocked.

Radio/cassette player can be operated.

Position 'II'

All instruments, warning lights and electrical circuits are operational.

Position 'III'

Starter motor operates.

Release the key immediately the engine starts (the key will automatically return to position 'II').

Note that operation of position 'I' electrical functions will be interrupted during engine cranking.

STARTING - DIESEL ENGINES

FOR VEHICLES EQUIPPED WITH A CATALYTIC CONVERTER:
Catalytic converters are easily damaged through improper use, particularly if the wrong fuel is used, or if an engine misfire occurs.

Before starting the engine and driving, ENSURE you are familiar with the precautions shown under 'Catalytic converter' later in this section.

In particular, you should be aware that continued use of the starter will result in unused fuel damaging the catalytic converter.

1. Check that the handbrake is applied and that the gear lever is in neutral.

2. Switch off all unnecessary electrical equipment.

3. Insert the starter key and turn the switch to position 'II'. Wait until the cold start warning light extinguishes.

NOTE: *When restarting a warm engine, it will not be necessary to wait for the cold start warning light to extinguish.*

4. Turn the key to position 'III' to operate the starter motor; DO NOT press the accelerator pedal during starting, and RELEASE THE KEY as soon as the engine is running.

NOTE: *In temperate climates, the battery charging and oil pressure warning lights should extinguish as soon as the engine is running.*

In cold weather, or when the battery is in a low state of charge, depress the clutch pedal while starting and hold it down until the engine is running.

In temperate climates, DO NOT operate the starter for longer than 10 seconds; if the engine fails to start, switch off and wait 10 seconds before re-using the starter. Please note that prolonged use of the starter will not only discharge the battery but may also damage the starter motor.

Cold climates

In very cold climates, the battery charging and oil pressure warning lights may take several seconds to extinguish. Similarly, engine cranking times will also increase; at -30° C the starter motor may need to be operated continuously for as long as 30 seconds before the engine will start. For this reason, ensure that all non-essential electrical equipment is switched off.

Warming up

In the interests of fuel economy, it is advisable to start driving straight away, remembering that harsh acceleration or labouring the engine before the normal operating temperature has been reached can damage the engine.

WARNING

The engine must not be run above fast idle speed until the oil pressure warning light extinguishes to ensure that the engine and turbo-charger bearings (Tdi models) are properly lubricated before being run at speed.

WARNING

Exhaust fumes contain poisonous substances which can cause unconsciousness and may even be fatal.

- *DO NOT inhale exhaust gases.*

- *DO NOT start or leave the engine running in an enclosed unventilated area, or drive with the rear door open.*

- *DO NOT modify the exhaust system from the original design.*

- *DO repair exhaust system or body leaks immediately.*

- *If you think exhaust fumes are entering the vehicle have the cause determined and corrected immediately.*

Switching off

To avoid the possibility of damaging the turbo-charger bearings (Tdi models) through inadequate lubrication, ALWAYS allow the engine to idle for 10 seconds before switching off. Turn the engine off by returning the starter switch to position 'I' and then position '0' to remove key.

STARTING - PETROL ENGINES

1. Check that the handbrake is applied and that the gear lever is in neutral.

2. Switch off all unnecessary electrical equipment.

3. If the engine is cold, pull out the cold start control (if fitted) and turn it clockwise to lock (see illustration).

4. Insert the starter key and turn the switch to position 'II' and then on to position 'III' to operate the starter motor. DO NOT press the accelerator pedal during starting and RELEASE THE KEY as soon as the engine is running.

In temperate climates DO NOT operate the starter for longer than 10 seconds. If the engine fails to start, switch off and wait 10 seconds before re-using the starter. Please note that prolonged use of the starter will not only discharge the battery but may also damage the starter motor.

In temperate climates, the battery charging and oil pressure warning lights should extinguish as soon as the engine is running.

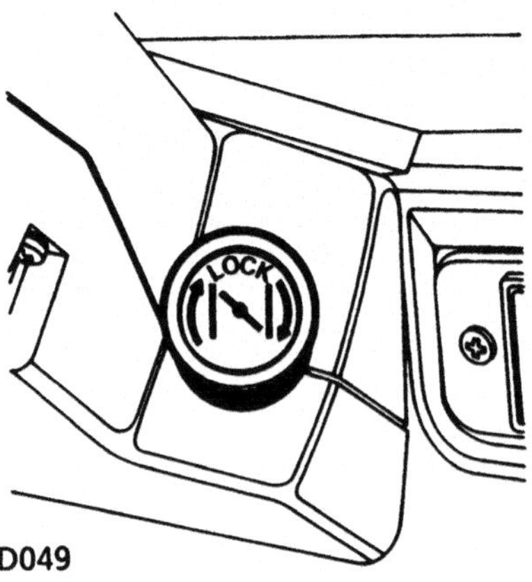

D049

In cold weather, or when the battery is in a low state of charge, depress the clutch pedal while starting and hold it down until the engine is running.

Cold climates

In very cold climates, the battery charging and oil pressure warning lights may take several seconds to extinguish. Similarly, engine cranking times will also increase; at -30° C the starter motor may need to be operated continuously for as long as 30 seconds before the engine will start. For this reason, ensure that all non-essential electrical equipment is switched off.

Additionally, in very cold climates, use of a cylinder block heater will improve the engine's starting characteristics. Your Land Rover dealer can advise you about the supply and use of a cylinder block heater.

Warming up

In the interests of fuel economy, it is advisable to start driving straight away, remembering that harsh acceleration or labouring the engine before the normal operating temperature has been reached can damage the engine.

NOTE: *Remember to turn off the cold start control once normal operating temperature is reached.*

WARNING

Exhaust fumes contain poisonous substances which can cause unconsciousness and may even be fatal.

- *DO NOT inhale exhaust gases.*

- *DO NOT start or leave the engine running in an enclosed unventilated area, or drive with the rear door open.*

- *DO NOT modify the exhaust system from the original design.*

- *DO repair exhaust system or body leaks immediately.*

- *If you think exhaust fumes are entering the vehicle have the cause determined and corrected immediately.*

Parking

After bringing the vehicle to a stop, ALWAYS apply the handbrake and select neutral in the main gearbox before releasing the footbrake and switching off the engine.

Switching off

Return the starter switch to position 'I' and then to position '0' to remove the key.

RUNNING-IN (petrol & diesel models)

Proper running-in will have a direct bearing on the reliability and smooth running of your vehicle throughout its life.

In particular, the engine, gearbox, brakes and tyres need time to bed-in and adjust to the demands of everyday motoring. It is therefore essential to drive with consideration for the running-in process for at least the first 800 km (500 miles) and observe the following advice:

- LIMIT maximum speed to 80 km/h (50 mph) for 4-cylinder engines and 95 km/h (60 mph) for V8 engines. Initially, drive the vehicle on a light throttle and only increase engine speeds once the running-in distance has been completed.

- DO NOT operate at full throttle or allow the engine to labour in any gear.

- AVOID fast acceleration and heavy braking except in emergencies.

EMISSION CONTROL SYSTEM

Land Rover vehicles are fitted with emission and evaporative control equipment necessary to meet a number of territorial requirements.

In many countries, it is against the law for vehicle owners to modify or tamper with emission control equipment, or to sanction the unauthorised replacement or modification of this equipment by a repair shop. In such cases, the vehicle owner and the repairer may both be liable for legal penalties.

It is important to remember that only Land Rover dealers are properly equipped to perform repairs and to maintain the emission control system on your vehicle.

FUEL ECONOMY

Fuel consumption is influenced by two major factors:

* How your vehicle is maintained.

* How you drive your vehicle.

To obtain optimum fuel economy, it is essential that your vehicle is maintained in accordance with the manufacturer's service schedule.

Items such as ignition timing, the condition of the air cleaner element, tyre pressures and wheel alignment can have a significant effect on fuel consumption. But above all, the way in which you drive is most important. The following hints may help you to obtain even better value from your motoring:

* Avoid unnecessary, short, start-stop journeys.

* Avoid fast starts by accelerating gently and smoothly from rest.

* Do not drive in the lower gears longer than necessary.

* Decelerate gently and avoid sudden and heavy braking.

* Anticipate obstructions and adjust your speed accordingly well in advance.

DRIVE GENTLY - SAVE FUEL!

IMPORTANT DRIVING INFORMATION
Instruments & warning lights

Before driving, it is important to fully understand the function of the instruments and warning lights described in section 2.

NOTE: Red warning lights are of particular importance, illumination indicates that a fault exists. If a red light illuminates, always stop the vehicle and seek qualified assistance before continuing.

Vehicle stability

Your vehicle has a higher ground clearance and, therefore, a higher centre of gravity than ordinary passenger cars. This will result in different handling characteristics.
Inexperienced drivers should take additional care, particularly in off-road driving situations and when performing abrupt manoeuvres at inappropriate speeds or on unstable surfaces.

Vehicle height

The overall height of your vehicle exceeds that of ordinary passenger cars. Always be aware of the height of your vehicle and check the available headroom before driving through low entrances. This is particularly important if the vehicle is fitted with a roof rack or if the sunroof is open.

Power assisted steering

Power assistance is progressively applied the more the steering wheel is turned. For example; where manual steering effort would normally be greatest (at slow speeds on maximum lock), power assistance is greatest. Similarly, where only minimal steering effort would normally be required (at high speed with the wheels straight ahead), then power assistance is also minimal, thus enabling the driver to benefit from apparently consistent steering effort at all times.

WARNING

Under no circumstances must the steering wheel be held on full lock for more than thirty seconds in one minute, otherwise the steering assembly may be damaged.

NOTE: Power assistance is dependent on the engine running. If the engine is not running, greater effort will be required to steer the vehicle.

Tdi engines

If a radiator blind is fitted, it must not obscure the intercooler section otherwise engine performance would be adversely affected. If in doubt, contact a Land Rover dealer.

Auxiliary equipment

WARNING

DO NOT use auxiliary equipment, such as roller generators, that are driven by one wheel of the vehicle, as they could cause failure of the gearbox differential. If the gearbox differential lock is engaged in an attempt to avoid damage, the vehicle will drive itself forward.

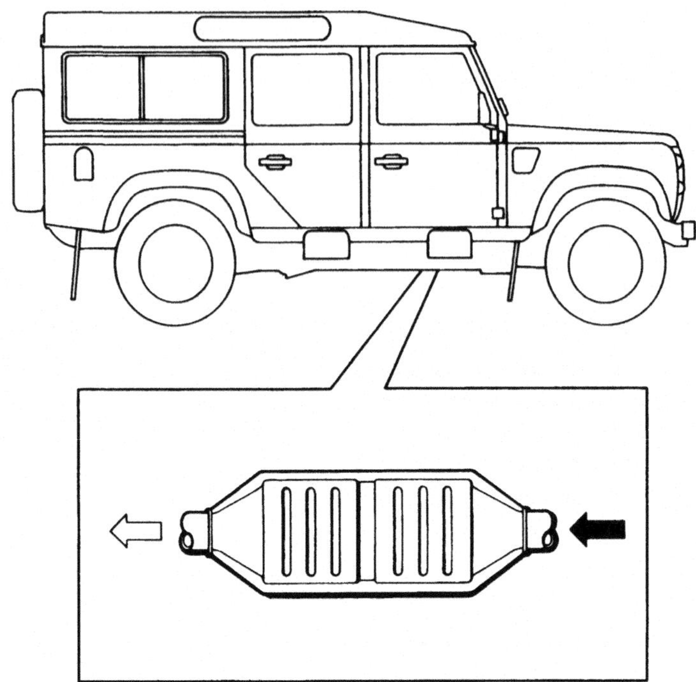

D050

CATALYTIC CONVERTER - (if fitted)

The exhaust system on some models of the Defender, incorporates a catalytic converter, which converts poisonous exhaust emissions from the engine into environmentally less harmful gases, thereby reducing atmospheric pollution.

The catalytic converter can be easily damaged through improper use, particularly if the wrong fuel is used, or if an engine misfire occurs. For this reason it is VERY IMPORTANT that you heed the precautions which follow:

Fuel

- Use ONLY fuel recommended for your vehicle.

Starting the engine

- DO NOT continue operating the starter if the engine fails to start after a few attempts (unburnt fuel may be drawn into the exhaust system, thereby poisoning the catalyst) - seek qualified assistance.

- When starting a COLD engine, DO NOT drive if a misfire is suspected - seek qualified assistance.

Driving

- Provided the engine has reached its normal operating temperature, if a misfire is suspected or the vehicle lacks power while driving, it may be driven SLOWLY (at risk of damaging the catalyst) to a Land Rover dealer for assistance.

- NEVER allow the vehicle to run out of fuel (the resultant misfire could destroy the catalyst).

- Engines burning excessive oil (blue smoke from the exhaust) will progressively reduce catalyst efficiency.

- On rough terrain, DO NOT allow the underside of the vehicle to be subjected to heavy impacts which could damage the catalytic converter.

- DO NOT overload or excessively rev the engine.

WARNING

Exhaust system temperatures can be extremely high - DO NOT park on ground where combustible materials such as dry grass or leaves could come into contact with the exhaust system (in dry weather a fire could result).

Switching off

- DO NOT switch off the engine while a forward or reverse gear is selected or whilst the vehicle is in motion.

Vehicle maintenance

- Any engine misfire, loss of engine performance or engine run-on, could seriously damage the catalytic converter. For this reason, it is vital that unqualified persons do not tamper with the engine, and that regular systematic maintenance is carried out by a Land Rover dealer.

PETROL ENGINES

USE ONLY RECOMMENDED FUEL

4 cylinder engines:
Use 90 RON minimum leaded or unleaded fuel wherever possible.

V8 engines:
Use 91 - 93 leaded or unleaded fuel wherever possible.

NOTE: *For petrol engined vehicles fitted with a catalytic converter, 95 RON minimum unleaded fuel MUST be used - leaded fuel will seriously damage the catalyst.*

The RON value (octane rating) of petroleum commonly available at garage forecourts will vary in different countries. The RON value quoted is the MINIMUM requirement and whilst this can be safely exceeded, no advantage in performance or fuel economy will be gained by using a higher octane fuel.

If heavy engine knock is detected when using the recommended octane rated fuel, or if steady engine knocking is present while maintaining a steady speed on level roads, contact your dealer for advice.

NOTE: *An occasional, light, engine knock while accelerating or climbing hills is acceptable.*

DIESEL ENGINES

The quality of diesel fuel (Derv) can vary in different countries and only clean, good quality fuel should be used. It is important that the sulphur content of diesel fuel does not exceed 1%; in Europe all supplies should be within this limit, but in other parts of the world, you should check with your supplier. Ensure the fuel filter element is changed at the recommended service intervals and clean the sediment bowl regularly (see 'Owner maintenance').

NOTE: *The use of paraffin (kerosene) as a diesel fuel additive is illegal in the UK.*

WARNING

On both petrol and diesel engine vehicles, if the fuel tank is accidentally filled with the wrong fuel, it is ESSENTIAL that you contact your dealer BEFORE attempting to start the engine!

Fuel

Fuel filling

WARNING

To avoid any sudden discharge of fuel caused by excessive air pressure, the cap is designed to allow the fuel tank to vent during the first half turn. DO NOT fully remove the cap until pressure has been released.

Filling station pumps are equipped with automatic cut-off sensing to avoid fuel spillage - only fill the tank until the filler nozzle automatically shuts off. DO NOT attempt to fill the tank beyond this point or spillage could result due to expansion of the fuel.

WARNING

DO NOT fully fill the tank if the vehicle is to be parked on a slope in direct sunlight or high ambient temperature - expansion of the fuel could cause spillage.

Empty fuel tank

DO NOT RUN THE FUEL TANK DRY!
In the case of vehicles equipped with a catalytic converter, running the fuel tank dry could create an engine misfire capable of damaging the catalytic converter.

In the case of diesel models, qualified assistance may be required to prime the fuel system before the engine can be restarted.

SAFETY ON THE FORECOURT
Petroleum gases are highly inflammable and in confined spaces are also explosive. Always take sensible precautions when refuelling:

- Switch off the engine.
- Do not smoke or use a naked flame or light.
- Take care not to spill fuel.
- Do not overfill the tank.

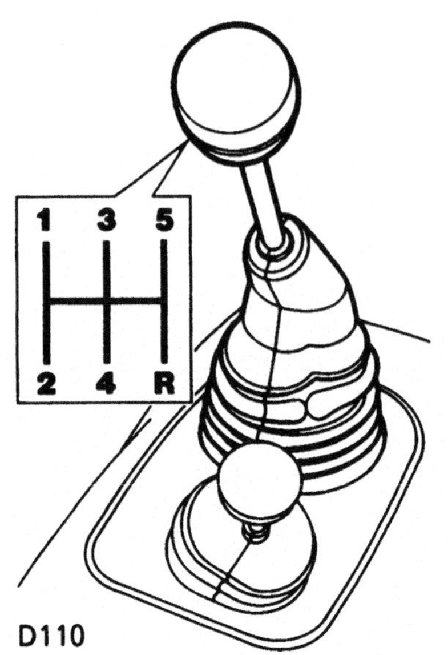

Clutch

Take care NOT to use the clutch pedal as a foot rest. To prevent unnecessary wear, always keep the left foot well clear of the clutch pedal, except when changing gear.

WARNING

Do NOT select reverse gear unless the vehicle is stationary.

MAIN GEARBOX

Your vehicle features a five speed main gearbox and a two speed transfer box. In addition, a centre differential in the transfer box distributes the drive to the front and rear axles, providing permanent four wheel drive. By using the main gearbox in conjunction with the transfer gears, ten forward and two reverse speeds are available.

The gear positions for the main gearbox are shown on the gear lever knob. Note that when the gearbox is in neutral, the gear lever is spring-loaded to automatically align between third and fourth gear positions.

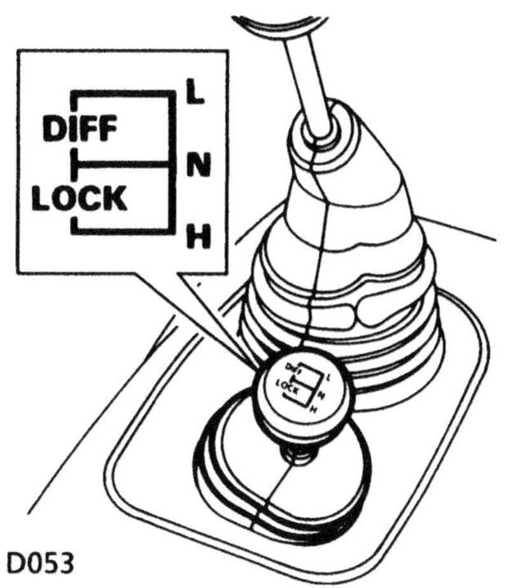

D053

TRANSFER GEARBOX

The second gear lever is used to select either the high or low range of gears in the transfer gearbox and, in addition, also controls the centre differential (known as the 'DIFF LOCK').

High range ('H')

Use high range for all normal road driving and also for off-road driving across dry, level terrain.

Low range ('L')

Use low range gears when moving off from rest when towing a heavy load, or in any situation where low speed manoeuvring is necessary, such as reversing a trailer or negotiating a boulder strewn river bed; also use for more extreme off-road conditions where progress in high range cannot be maintained.

Neutral ('N')

With the transfer lever in neutral, drive cannot be transmitted to the road wheels, regardless of the position of the main gear lever. Use transfer neutral when being towed or when using winching or power take off facilities.

'Diff lock' centre differential

Use the 'unlocked' position for all normal driving, and use the 'DIFF-LOCK' position to improve traction in extreme conditions where wheel grip could be lost, such as: wet grass, mud, sand, ice or snow. Return to the 'unlocked' position as soon as dry, firm, ground is reached.

DO NOT use the 'diff lock' unnecessarily!

USING THE TRANSFER GEARBOX

With the vehicle stationary and the engine running, depress the clutch and then move the lever fully forward (or backwards) in TWO distinct but positive moves - 'high to neutral'.... 'neutral to low' (or vice versa).

If there is resistance to the gear engaging, do not force the lever. Instead, with the main lever in gear, release the clutch momentarily and then try again.

Changing from low to high on the move:
Changing from 'L' (low) to 'H' (high) can be achieved without stopping the vehicle, as follows:

1. Apply slight backward pressure to the transfer gear lever in preparation for changing.

2. Then, in three simultaneous moves, depress the clutch, release the accelerator and pull the transfer lever into neutral.

3. Release the clutch pedal for approximately 3 seconds before depressing it again and moving the transfer lever firmly into the high position.

4. Finally, select a suitable main gear, release the clutch and continue driving in the normal way.

NOTE: *After a little practice, this operation can be carried out smoothly and quickly by using firm, positive moves.*

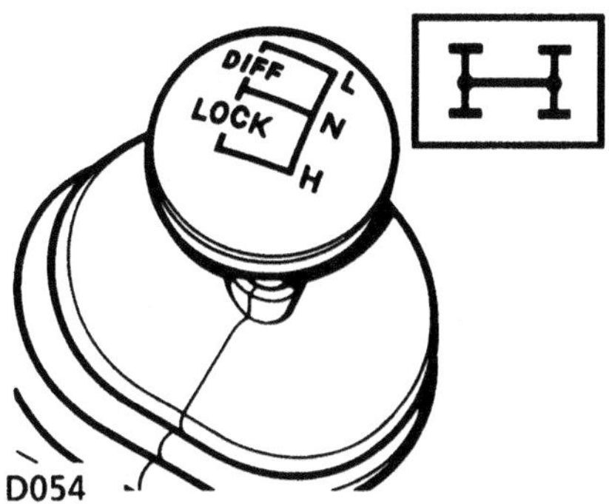

THE DIFFERENTIAL LOCK

Unlike other four wheel drive vehicles, all Land Rover vehicles have permanent four wheel drive. This is achieved by the inclusion of a lockable differential between the front and rear drive shafts. With the differential locked, the drive shafts to front and rear axles are (in effect) joined together, causing both to rotate at the same speed. This is a normal feature with all four wheel drive vehicles and enhances traction on difficult off-road surfaces. However, with the differential unlocked the different running requirements of the two axles can be accommodated, thereby enabling Land Rover vehicles to operate permanently in four wheel drive for both normal AND off-road use.

Selecting diff lock

The diff lock can be engaged or disengaged either with the vehicle stationary, or when driving at any road speed. However, with the vehicle in motion it is ESSENTIAL to be travelling on firm ground, in a straight line, and without wheel slip.

> **WARNING**
>
> *DO NOT engage the diff lock if one or more wheels are slipping - this could damage the transmission. If wheels are slipping, ease off the accelerator before engaging the diff lock.*
>
> *DO NOT engage the diff lock from the transfer neutral position.*

To lock the differential:

Briefly ease the throttle and depress the clutch while moving the transfer gear lever to the left - from either 'H' (high) or 'L' (low) position. Release the clutch as soon as the differential is locked (the warning light on the instrument panel will illuminate).

To unlock the differential:

Move the transfer gear lever to the right - to either 'H' (high) or 'L' (low) position as required; when the diff lock disengages the warning light will extinguish.

Gearbox & transmission

When to use the diff lock

As a general rule, the differential should only be locked in order to drive off-road on loose and slippery surfaces. ALWAYS unlock the differential for normal road driving or as soon as a hard grippy surface is reached whether high or low gears are selected.

NOTE: *A valuable introduction to off-road driving, which includes many useful references to the transfer gearbox and 'diff lock', is included in the 'Off-road driving' section of the handbook.*

WARNING

If the vehicle is driven on normal road surfaces with the differential locked, the steering will feel stiff, excessive tyre wear will occur and the transmission will be 'wound up'. This places excessive strain on the transmission.

Diff lock warning light

The amber warning light on the instrument panel illuminates when the diff lock is actually engaged - rather than when it has been selected. Similarly it will only extinguish when the diff lock is actually disengaged. This accounts for a slight delay between diff lock disengagement and the warning light extinguishing which is quite normal.

IMPORTANT INFORMATION

Transmission 'wind up'

If the warning light is obviously reluctant to extinguish after the diff lock has disengaged, some transmission 'wind up' may be present.

Reversing the vehicle for a short distance and then going forward will usually 'unwind' the transmission and extinguish the light and the vehicle can then be driven as normal. However, if after two or three attempts to 'unwind' the transmission the light remains on, consult your dealer AS SOON AS POSSIBLE.

Brakes

BRAKING SYSTEM

As a safety precaution, the hydraulic braking system operates through dual circuits. If one circuit fails, the other will continue to function, but increased brake pedal travel and longer stopping distances will be experienced.

Servo assistance

The braking system is servo assisted, but ONLY when the engine is running. Without this assistance, greater braking effort is necessary to safely control the vehicle, resulting in longer stopping distances. Always observe the following precautions:

- NEVER allow the vehicle to freewheel with the engine turned off.

- ALWAYS take particular care when being towed with the engine turned off.

- If the engine should stop for any reason while the vehicle is in motion, bring the vehicle to a halt as quickly as traffic conditions safely allow, and DO NOT pump the brake pedal as the braking system may lose any remaining assistance available.

Brake pads

Brake pads require a period of bedding in. You should avoid heavy braking, except in emergencies, for at least the first 800 km (500 miles).

Remember that regular servicing is vital to ensure that the brake pads are examined for wear and changed periodically to ensure long term safety and optimum performance.

WARNING

DO NOT rest your foot on the brake pedal while travelling, as this may overheat the brakes, reduce their efficiency and cause excessive wear.

NEVER move a vehicle without the engine running because braking assistance will not be available. The pedal brakes will still function, but more pressure will be required.

ALWAYS take particular care when being towed with the engine turned off.

If the brake warning light should illuminate while the vehicle is in motion, bring the vehicle to a halt as quickly as traffic conditions and safety permit and seek qualified assistance before continuing - DO NOT pump the brake pedal. If the brake pedal is pumped, the braking system may lose any remaining assistance available.

Wet conditions

Driving through water or even very heavy rain may adversely affect braking efficiency. Always dry the braking surfaces by intermittent light application of the brakes, first ensuring that you are at a safe distance from other road users.

HANDBRAKE

Unlike most other vehicles, the handbrake operates on the rear propeller shaft, and NOT on the road wheels. This may result in slight movement of the vehicle after the handbrake is applied.

To engage the handbrake, depress the button and pull the lever up.

To release, pull the lever up slightly, depress the button and lower the lever.

Always apply the handbrake fully whenever you park.

When parking on a slope, do not rely on the handbrake alone to hold the vehicle, park in a low forward gear when facing uphill and in reverse gear when facing downhill. For extra security on steep slopes, move the transfer lever into low range or engage the diff lock.

WARNING

DO NOT apply the handbrake while the vehicle is in motion as this could result in loss of vehicle control and damage to the transmission.

DO NOT rely on the handbrake to operate effectively if the vehicle has been subjected to immersion in mud and water (see 'Off-road driving').

TOWING

The torque ranges of Land Rover engines allow maximum-weight loads to be pulled smoothly from standstill, and reduce gear changing on hills or rough terrain.

The suspension is designed to cope with a heavy trailer load without upsetting the balance or feel of the vehicle.

WARNING

Only fit towing accessories that have been designed and approved by Land Rover.

Ensure that the gross weight and maximum rear axle weight are not exceeded.

When preparing your vehicle for towing, always pay careful attention to the trailer manufacturer's recommendations and the following guidelines.

- Ensure that the towing vehicle tyre pressures are correct and that the trailer tyre pressures are as recommended by the trailer manufacturer.

- With the trailer and vehicle unladen, balance the combination so that the trailer draw-bar and the hitch point on the vehicle are at the same height. Adjust the height of the hitch point if necessary.

- Check the operation of trailer brakes and lights.

- For maximum stability, ensure that loads are properly secured and unable to shift position during transit. Also, position loads so that most of the weight is placed close to the floor and, where possible, immediately above or close to the trailer axle(s).

- After loading the trailer, check that the weight on the hitch point (this is called the draw-bar loading weight, or nose weight), is in accordance with the manufacturer's recommendations.

- When calculating the laden weight of the trailer, remember to include the weight of the trailer PLUS THE LOAD.

- Where the load weight can be divided between trailer and tow vehicle, loading more weight into the vehicle will generally improve the stability of the combination.

- A smooth start will be achieved with trailers over 2000 kg (4400 lb) by moving off in LOW range, then changing to HIGH range while on the move (see 'Transfer gearbox').

NOTE: *Towing regulations vary from country to country. It is very important to ensure that national regulations governing towing weights and speed limits are observed (refer to the relevant national motoring organisation for information). The following maximum permissible towed weights refer to the vehicle's design limitations and NOT to any specific territorial restriction.*

Maximum permissible towed weights	On-road kg	Off-road kg
Unbraked trailers	750	500
Trailers with overrun brakes	3500	1000
4 wheel trailers with coupled brakes		
Petrol and Diesel (turbo)	4000	1000
Diesel (non-turbo)	3500	1000

NOSE WEIGHT

The recommended trailer nose weight limit is 75 kg (165 lb). The nose weight plus the combined weight of the vehicle's load carrying area and rear seat passengers, must never exceed the maximum rear axle load or the gross vehicle weight (as shown in 'General data').

WARNING

DO NOT carry unsecured equipment, tools or luggage which could move and cause personal injury in the event of an accident or emergency manoeuvre, either on or off road.

VEHICLE WEIGHTS

When loading a vehicle to its maximum (gross vehicle weight), consideration must be taken of the unladen vehicle weight and the distribution of the load to ensure that axle loadings do not exceed the permitted maximum values.

It is your responsibility to limit the vehicle load in such a way that neither the maximum axle loads nor the gross vehicle weight are exceeded (see 'General data').

Coupled braking systems

In order to tow a trailer with a weight in excess of 3,500 kg, the vehicle must be adapted to operate a coupled brake system. If this adaptation is carried out, the vehicle identification number plate (VIN) must be changed to show the increased train weight.

Revised VIN plates may be obtained from Land Rover; these will be issued subject to satisfactory proof that the vehicle has been fitted with an approved conversion.

NOTE: Above 300 metres (1,000 feet) the effects of altitude can adversely affect engine performance and also cause overheating.

Trailer socket

When the engine is running, power consumption from trailer socket must NOT exceed 5 amps.

ROOF RACK

ALWAYS use an approved roof rack and follow the manufacturers' fitting instructions carefully. A full list of all available accessories is available from your Land Rover dealer.

WARNING

ALWAYS consult your dealer for advice regarding the approval, suitability, installation and use of any parts or accessories before fitting.

IMPORTANT INFORMATION

- The MAXIMUM roof rack load is 75 kg.

- A loaded roof rack can reduce the stability of the vehicle, particularly when cornering and encountering cross winds.

- All loads should be evenly distributed, and secured within the periphery of the rack.

- Always secure the load to the side rails, not just to the cross rails.

- Only fit roof racks that have been designed for your vehicle. If in doubt, consult your dealer.

Emergency starting

Starting an engine with a discharged battery

The ONLY recommended methods of restarting a vehicle with a discharged battery are:

- The use of a substitute battery fitted to the disabled vehicle.

- The use of booster cables to connect the battery from a donor vehicle to the discharged battery.

USING BOOSTER CABLES

WARNING

Batteries emit explosive hydrogen gas - keep sparks and naked lights away from the battery compartment.

Make sure BOTH batteries are of the same voltage (12 volts), and that the booster cables have insulated clamps and are approved for use with 12 volt batteries.

DO NOT connect positive (+) terminals to negative (-) terminals, and ensure booster cables are kept away from any moving parts in the engine compartment.

Take care when working near rotating parts of the engine.

Always adopt the following procedure when using booster cables:.

1. If a donor vehicle is to be used, both vehicles should be parked with their battery locations adjacent to each other. Ensure that the two vehicles do not touch.

2. Apply the handbrakes and ensure that the transmission of both vehicles is set in neutral ('P' or Park for donor vehicles with automatic transmission).

3. Turn off the starter switch and ALL electrical equipment of BOTH vehicles.

4. Connect the RED booster cable between the positive (+) terminal of the donor battery and the positive (+) terminal of the discharged battery.

5. Connect the BLACK booster cable from the negative (-) terminal of the donor battery to a good earthing point on the disabled vehicle (eg. an engine mounting, chassis member or other unpainted metal surface) - remote from the battery and well away from fuel and brake lines. **For safety reasons, DO NOT connect this cable to the negative terminal of the discharged battery.**

6. Check that the booster cables are clear of any moving parts in either engine, then start the engine of the donor vehicle and allow it to idle for a few minutes.

7. Now start the vehicle with the discharged battery.

8. Once both engines are running normally, allow them to idle for two minutes before switching off the engine of the donor vehicle and disconnecting the booster cables. DO NOT switch on any electrical circuits on the previously disabled vehicle until AFTER the booster cables have been removed.

9. Disconnecting the booster cables must be an EXACT reversal of the connecting procedure, **ie; disconnect the BLACK cable from the earthing point on the disabled vehicle FIRST.**

Vehicle recovery

VEHICLE RECOVERY

If it is necessary to recover the vehicle by towing, always adhere to the following procedure:

Towing the vehicle (on four-wheels)

1. Set the main gearbox and transfer box in neutral.

2. Ensure the differential lock is in the unlocked position.

3. Turn the starter switch to the first position to unlock the steering and leave in this position while the vehicle is being towed.

4. Secure the towing attachment to the vehicle.

5. Release the handbrake.

NOTE: If, due to an accident or electrical fault it is not considered safe to turn the starter switch, the battery must be disconnected.

IMPORTANT INFORMATION

DO NOT attempt to tow the vehicle unless the starter switch is turned to position 'I' (to unlock the steering).

- DO NOT attempt to remove the starter key or turn the switch to position '0' while the vehicle is in motion.

- Without the engine running, the brake servo and power steering pump cannot provide assistance. Greater brake pedal and steering effort are therefore necessary to safely control the vehicle.

Suspended tow

WARNING

Your vehicle has permanent four wheel drive - the propeller shaft MUST be removed from the axle to be trailed.

If the front axle is to be trailed ALWAYS adhere to the following precautions:

- Ensure the four bolts securing the front propeller shaft to the gearbox are tightly secured with the appropriate nuts after disconnecting the propeller shaft - otherwise serious damage to the gearbox may occur.

- Unlock the steering.

- Secure the steering wheel and/or linkage in the straight ahead position - the steering lock MUST NOT be used for this purpose.

WARNING

The propeller shaft MUST only be reconnected by a qualified Land Rover engineer. Contact your Land Rover dealer for further information.

D057

Transporter or trailer lashing

Use the towing rings on the front and rear cross members as lashing points (see illustration). DO NOT secure lashing hooks or trailer fixings to any other part of the vehicle.

Ancillary equipment

Winches

A number of different winches, suited to jobs ranging from vehicle recovery to haulage, can be fitted to your Defender. For further information on the types of winch available and their various uses, contact your Land Rover dealer.

As winch operation will vary considerably on different winch units, it is essential that the manufacturer's operating instructions are understood and followed carefully.

Winch safety

> **WARNING**
>
> *If used incorrectly, winches can be extremely dangerous.*
>
> *ALWAYS follow the manufacturer's operating instructions carefully.*
>
> *NEVER stand near, or astride a winching cable whilst it is under tension.*
>
> *ALWAYS wear protective gloves when handling winching cables.*

In addition;

- DO NOT attempt to continue winching if the winch has stalled due to overloading.

- Inspect the winch and cable regularly - ALWAYS have worn or damaged parts replaced immediately.

- Only use recommended replacement parts of the same specification as the original equipment - failure to do so may not only damage the winch, but may cause serious personal injury.

After winching

Whilst wearing gloves, clean and grease the cable with an oily or greased cloth.

> **WARNING**
>
> *NEVER allow a cable to kink, coil or overlap.*

NOTE: *If a capstan winch is used, ensure the rope is cleaned and dried before stowing.*

Power take-off drives

Your Defender is capable of providing a static or mobile power source, which can be used to power generators, compressors, pumps and other ancillary equipment, mounted on or under the vehicle, by means of shaft, belt or hydraulic drive. This is possible by fitting a power take-off drive unit to the transfer gearbox. This provides the basic drive for several variations of power take-off layouts.

The power take-off capability is an integral part of the vehicle design and has been tried and tested under the most rigorous and demanding conditions across the world. Land Rover dealers provide a full range of power take-off drive units and accessories, designed and built for the Defender.

For static operation, select neutral in the transfer gearbox to disconnect the drive to the road wheels - it is then possible to operate the power take-off independently. The forward gears can now be used to control the operating speed. To prevent the transmission from being overloaded, it is recommended that the highest gear possible should be used.

The lower gears can be used when lower operating speeds are required, but they should only be used for light workloads and for short periods of time.

If power take-off is being used while the vehicle is moving, it will operate at a speed in direct proportion to the road speed of the vehicle and to the selected transfer gear ratio.

For more information on the use of power take-off drives and equipment, consult your Land Rover dealer.

SECTION 4
Owner maintenance

The long-term safety, reliability and performance of your vehicle will depend very largely on how well it is maintained.

Maintenance is the owner's responsibility and it is ESSENTIAL that all routine services are carried out by a Land Rover dealer at the specified intervals. These are shown in the Owner Information & Service Record book included in the literature pack. The Owner Information & Service Record book also includes service record dockets, which must be correctly endorsed by your Land Rover dealer at the conclusion of each service.

This section of the handbook includes information to assist the owner carry out those daily, weekly and monthly checks that are also necessary to ensure safe, reliable motoring.

Owner maintenance

OWNER MAINTENANCE

In addition to the routine services, which should be carried out by your Land Rover dealer at the intervals shown in the Owner Information & Service Record book, a number of simple checks (listed below) must be carried out by the owner or driver on a regular basis.
These are fully described on the pages that follow.

Daily checks

* Operation of lights, horn, direction indicators, wipers, washers and warning lights.

* Operation of seat belts and brakes.

* Look for deposits on the garage floor which may indicate a fluid leak.

Weekly checks

These should be carried out at least every 250 miles or 400 km.

* Engine oil level.

* Cooling system level.

* Screen washer reservoir level.

* Condition and pressure of tyres.

* Drain fuel sedimenter and filter - Diesel engines (if fitted).

Monthly checks

* Brake fluid level.

* Power steering fluid level.

NOTE: *Any significant or sudden drop in fluid levels, or uneven tyre wear should be reported to a Land Rover dealer without delay.*

The gearbox fluid level should only be checked by a Land Rover dealer at the time of a routine service. All fluid specifications and capacities are shown in 'General data'.

IMPORTANT INFORMATION

Special operating conditions

When a vehicle is operated in extremely arduous conditions or on dusty, wet or muddy terrain, more frequent attention must be paid to servicing requirements.

For example; if your vehicle experiences deep wading conditions, even DAILY servicing could be necessary to ensure the continued safe and reliable operation of the vehicle.

Contact a Land Rover dealer for advice.

Owner maintenance

Planned maintenance

Regular systematic maintenance is the key to ensuring the continued reliability and efficiency of your vehicle.

The routine maintenance requirements for your vehicle are shown in the Owner Information & Service Record book. Most of this necessary workshop maintenance requires specialised knowledge and equipment, and should preferably be entrusted to your Land Rover dealer.

Emission control

Your vehicle is fitted with various items of emission and evaporative control equipment designed to meet specific territorial requirements.

You should be aware that unauthorised replacement, modification or tampering with this equipment by an owner or repair shop, may be unlawful and subject to legal penalties.

In addition, engine settings must not be tampered with. These have been established to ensure that your vehicle complies with stringent exhaust emission regulations. Incorrect engine settings may adversely affect exhaust emissions, engine performance and fuel consumption, as well as causing high temperatures, which will result in damage to the catalytic converter (if fitted) and the vehicle.

Road testing on dynamometers ('rolling roads')

WARNING

Because your vehicle is equipped with permanent four-wheel drive, it is essential that any dynamometer testing is carried out ONLY by a qualified person familiar with the dynamometer testing and safety procedures practised by Land Rover dealers. Contact your Land Rover dealer for further information.

SAFETY IN THE GARAGE

Whenever you carry out maintenance on your vehicle, the following safety precautions should be observed at all times.

- ALWAYS keep hands, tools and items of clothing clear of all drive belts and pulleys.

- DO NOT touch exhaust or cooling system components until they are cool.

- DO NOT touch electrical leads or components with the starter switch turned on.

- NEVER leave the engine running in an unventilated area - exhaust gases are poisonous and contain carbon monoxide, which can cause unconsciousness and may even be fatal.

- DO NOT work beneath the vehicle with the wheel change lifting jack as the only means of support.

- Ensure sparks and naked lights are kept away from the engine and battery compartments.

WARNING

Remember; cooling fans and air conditioning system condenser fans (if fitted), may continue to operate after the engine is switched off. Always wait until the fans have completely stopped moving before working in the engine compartment.

Poisonous liquids

Most liquids and lubricants used in motor vehicles are poisonous and should not be consumed, or brought into contact with open wounds. These include: battery acid, anti-freeze, brake and power steering fluid, as well as petrol, diesel, engine oil and windscreen washer additives.

For your own safety, ALWAYS read and obey all instructions printed on labels and containers.

Used engine oil

Prolonged contact with engine oil can cause serious skin disorders, including dermatitis and skin cancer. ALWAYS wash thoroughly after contact.

It is illegal to pollute drains, water courses or soil with toxic chemicals such as used engine oil. ALWAYS dispose of vehicle liquids and lubricants, at authorised waste disposal sites or at garages which provide facilities for the receipt of used engine oil and toxic chemicals. If in doubt, contact your Local Authority for advice.

PROTECT THE ENVIRONMENT!

Bonnet opening

Ensure the wipers are switched off and have returned to the parked position before opening the bonnet.

On vehicles with a bonnet mounted spare wheel, the bonnet will be heavy to lift - DO NOT allow it to drop.

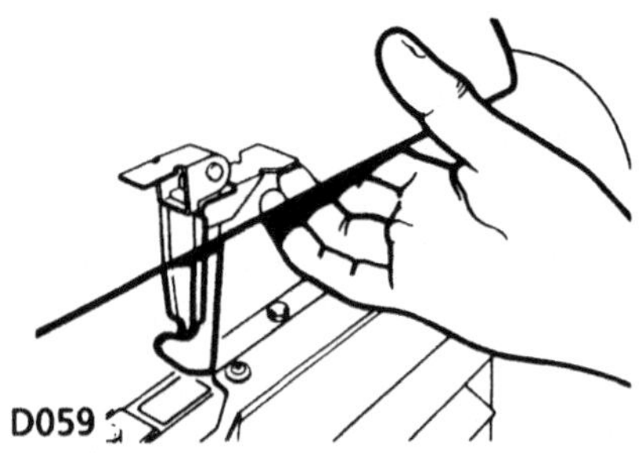

D059

Lift the safety catch lever (as illustration) and raise the bonnet.

Prop stay

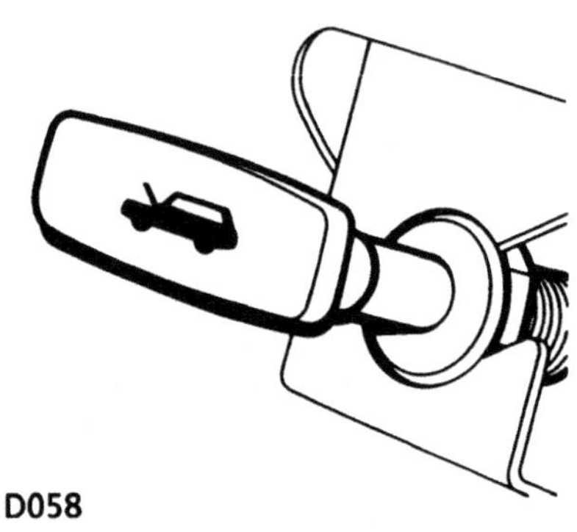

D058

Pull the bonnet release handle.

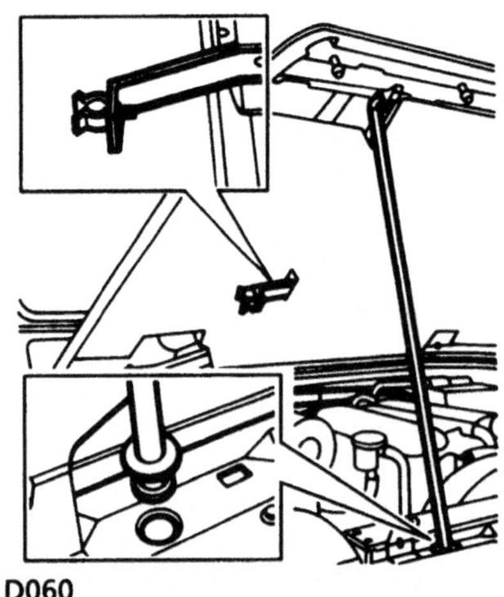

D060

Release the bonnet support stay from the underside of the bonnet and fit the stay in the corresponding hole in the bonnet locking platform.

Scissor action stay

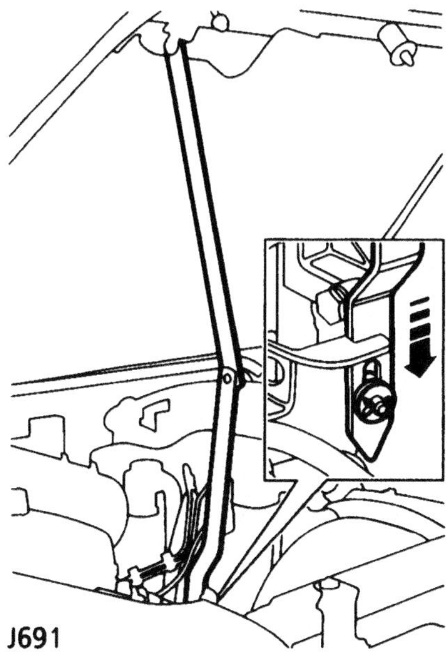

J691

Raise the bonnet until the stay fully extends.
Release the bonnet, ensuring that the stay
locks into position.

Closing the bonnet

After closing the bonnet, check that the lock is
fully engaged by attempting to lift the front
edge of the bonnet. This should be free from
all movement.

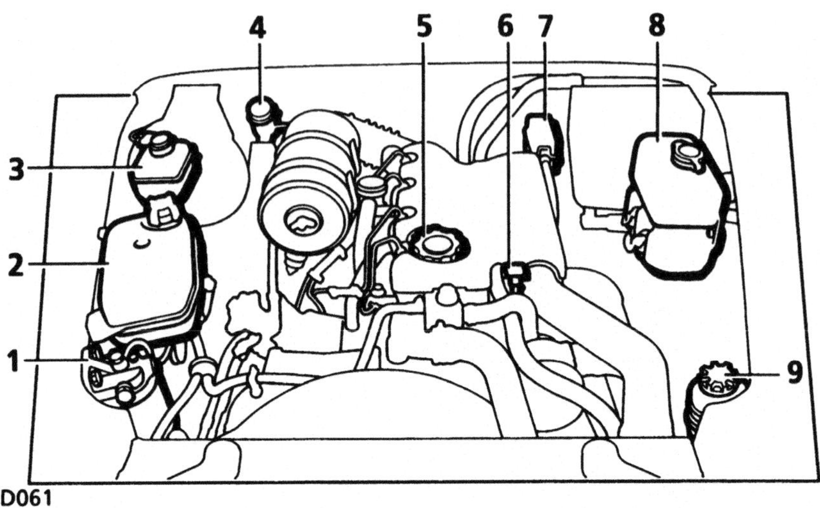

Tdi - Right hand steering

1. Diesel fuel filter.

2. Cooling system reservoir.

3. Brake fluid reservoir.

4. Clutch fluid reservoir.

5. Engine oil filler cap.

6. Engine oil dipstick.

7. Fuse box - engine compartment.

8. Washer reservoir.

9. Power steering reservoir.

WARNING

Ensure that sparks and naked lights are kept away from the engine compartment.

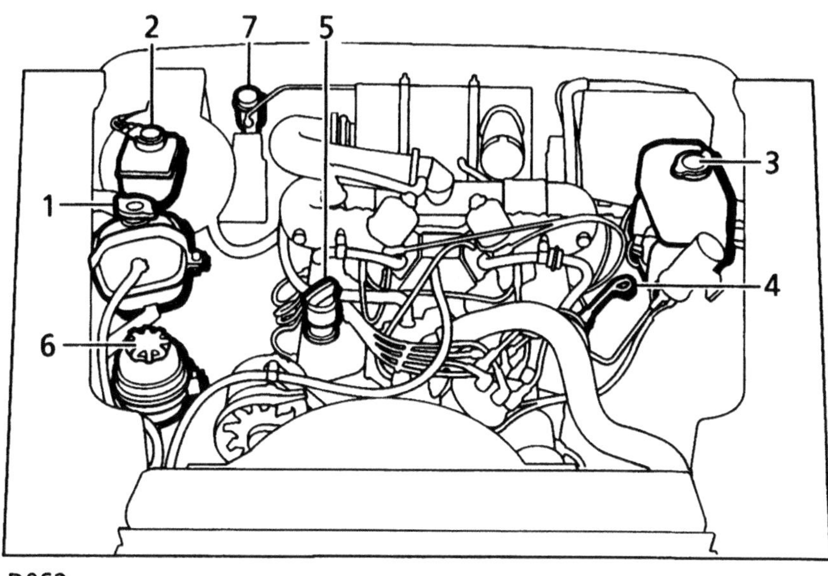

D062

V8 - Right hand steering

1. Cooling system reservoir
2. Brake fluid reservoir.
3. Washer reservoir.
4. Engine oil dipstick.
5. Engine oil filler cap.
6. Power steering reservoir.
7. Clutch fluid reservoir.

WARNING

Ensure that sparks and naked lights are kept away from the engine compartment.

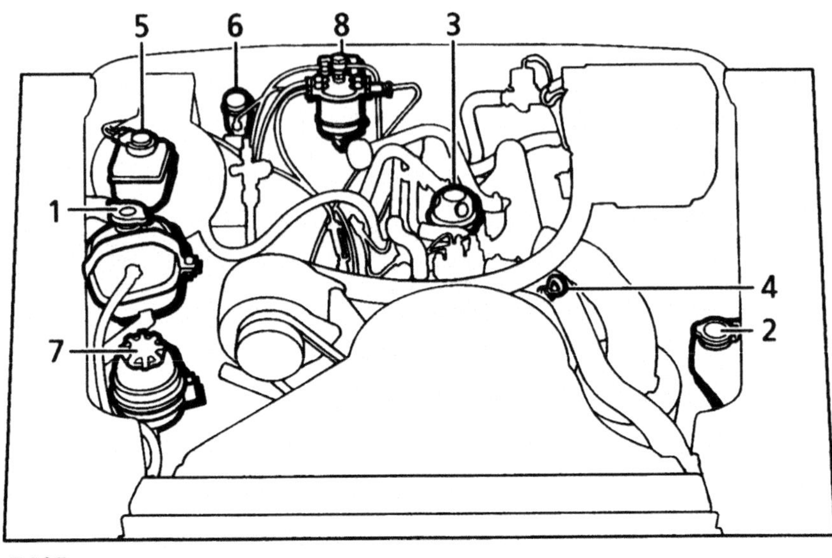

D105

4-cylinder diesel
(non turbo)

1. Cooling system reservoir.
2. Washer reservoir.
3. Engine oil filler cap.
4. Engine oil dipstick.
5. Brake fluid reservoir.
6. Clutch fluid reservoir.
7. Power steering reservoir.
8. Diesel fuel filter.

WARNING

Ensure that sparks and naked lights are kept away from the engine compartment.

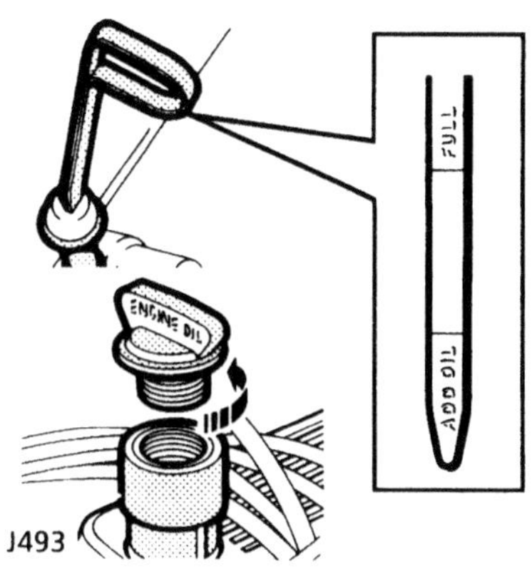

V8 Petrol engine

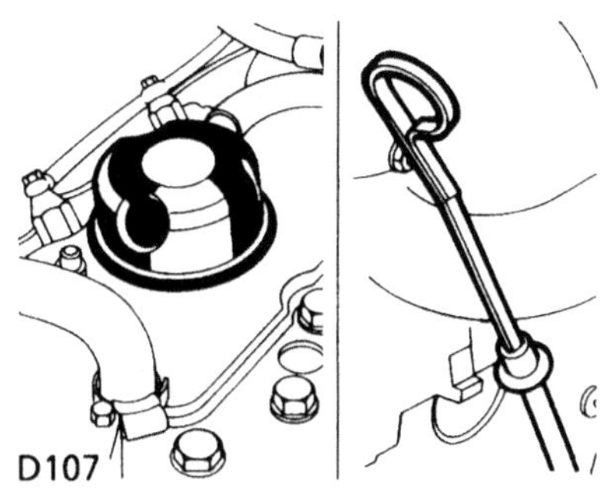

4-cylinder petrol and diesel (non-turbo)

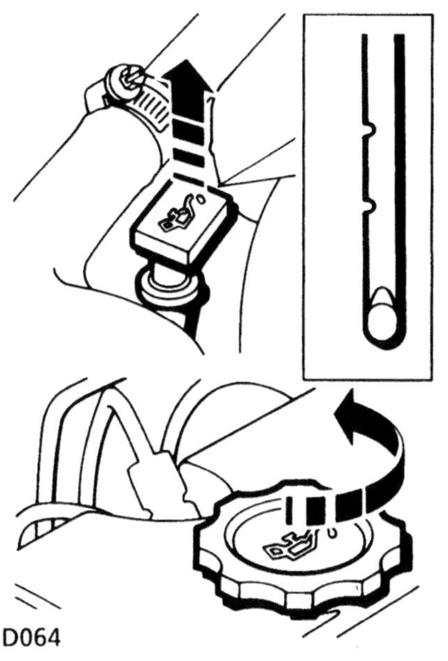

Tdi Diesel engine

ENGINE OIL LEVEL-CHECK & TOP-UP

Check the oil level at least every 400 km (250 miles) when the engine is HOT and with the vehicle resting on level ground.

Switch off the engine and let the vehicle stand for five minutes to allow the oil to drain back into the sump. Withdraw the dipstick and wipe the blade clean and then fully reinsert the dipstick and withdraw again to check the level, which should NEVER be allowed to fall below the lower mark on the dipstick.

To top-up, unscrew the oil filler cap and add oil to maintain the level between the UPPER and LOWER marks on the dipstick.

DO NOT OVERFILL!

As a general guide, if the level on the dipstick:

- is nearer to the upper mark than the lower, add no oil.

- is nearer to the lower mark than the upper, add half a litre of oil.

- is below the lower mark, add one litre of oil and re-check the level after a further five minutes.

NOTE: If it is necessary to check the oil level when the engine is cold, DO NOT start the engine. Follow the procedure detailed above, but re-check the oil level as soon as the engine has reached its normal operating temperature.

Oil specifications

It is essential to use an oil suitable for the climatic conditions in which the vehicle is to be operated. Precise specifications are shown in 'General data'. If in doubt, contact your Land Rover dealer.

COOLING SYSTEM TOP-UP

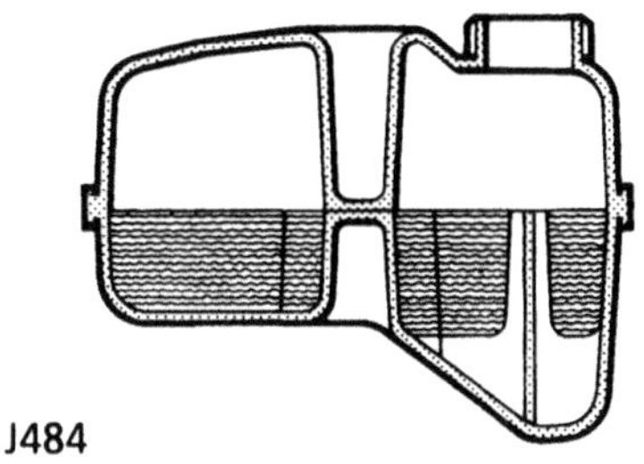

J484

NEVER remove the filler cap or radiator filler plug when the engine is hot - escaping steam or scalding water could cause serious injury.

The coolant level in the reservoir should be checked at least weekly (more frequently in high mileage or arduous operating conditions). Always check the level WHEN THE SYSTEM IS COLD.

Unscrew the filler cap slowly, allowing the pressure to escape before removing completely.

Never run the engine without coolant.

Top-up with a 50% mixture of anti-freeze and water so that the surface of the coolant is level with the seam on the side of the tank. Ensure the cap is tightened fully after top-up is completed.

DO NOT overfill. This may result in damage to the radiator.

If the level has fallen appreciably, suspect leakage or overheating and arrange for your dealer to examine your vehicle.

V8 models

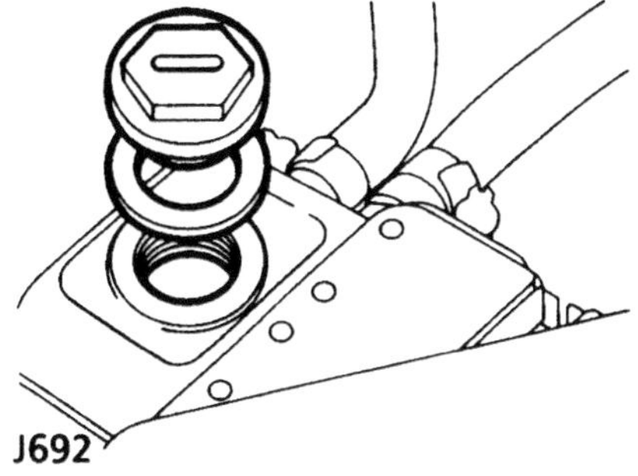

J692

On V8 models, as well as removing the reservoir cap, carefully unscrew the radiator filler plug (illustrated above), allowing pressure to escape before removing completely.

Top the radiator up, if necessary, with a 50% mixture of anti-freeze and water to maintain the level at approximately 12 mm (0.5 in) below the radiator filler neck. Ensure the plug is tightened fully after top-up is completed.

DO NOT OVERFILL!

Anti-freeze

Anti-freeze contains important corrosion inhibitors. Ensure the 50% anti-freeze/water solution is maintained and topped up all year round (not just in cold conditions). Failure to do so may cause corrosion of the radiator and engine components.

Use an ethylene glycol based anti-freeze (containing no methanol) with non-phosphate corrosion inhibitors suitable for use in aluminium engines. The specific gravity of a 50% anti-freeze solution at 68° F (20° C) is 1.075 and protects against frost down to -33° F (-36° C).

WARNING

Prevent anti-freeze coming in contact with the skin or eyes. If this occurs, rinse immediately with plenty of water.

Anti-freeze will damage painted surfaces.

NEVER top-up with salt water. Even when travelling in territories where the water supply contains salt, always ensure you carry a supply of fresh (rain or distilled) water.

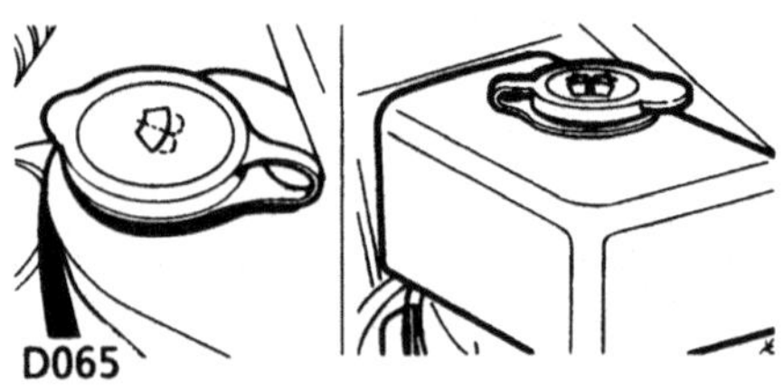

WINDSCREEN WASHER TOP-UP

The windscreen washer reservoir also supplies the rear screen.

Check the reservoir level and top-up with a mixture of water and an approved screen washer solvent to approximately 25 mm (1 in) below the bottom of the filler neck. In cold weather, to prevent freezing, use a screen washer solvent containing isopropanol.

Operate the washer switches to check that the nozzles are clear and properly directed.

WARNING

DO NOT use an anti-freeze solution in the washer reservoir. Anti-freeze will damage painted surfaces.

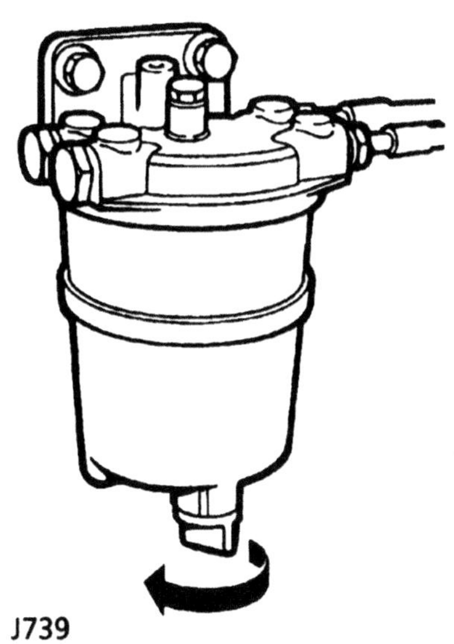

J739

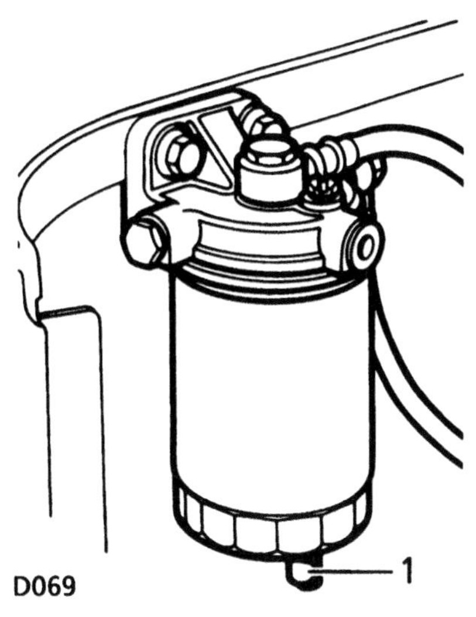

D069 —1

FUEL SEDIMENTER - diesel engines
(if fitted)

The sedimenter is located on the chassis side member, near the rear wheel.

To drain:

Slacken off the drain plug (arrowed in illustration), to allow any water to drain off. Retighten the plug as soon as pure diesel is emitted.

NOTE: If your vehicle is fitted with two fuel tanks, it may have two sedimenters - one on each side of the vehicle.

FUEL FILTER - diesel engines

The filter is located at the front of the engine compartment.

To drain:

Slacken off the drain plug (1), to allow any water to drain off. Retighten the plug as soon as pure diesel is emitted.

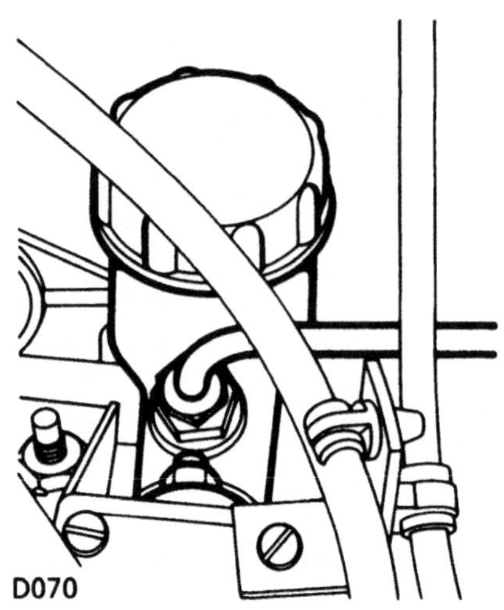

D070

CLUTCH FLUID TOP-UP

Wipe the filler cap before removing, to prevent dirt from entering the reservoir. Check the fluid level and top up if necessary, maintaining the level approximately 10 mm below the top of the reservoir, using fluid meeting *FMVSS 116 DOT 4* specification. Ensure dirt does not enter the reservoir while filling.

Use only new fluid from a sealed container (old fluid from opened containers, or fluid previously bled from the system must NOT be used).

DO NOT OVERFILL!

If significant topping up is required, a leak is indicated - consult your dealer immediately.

Engine compartment

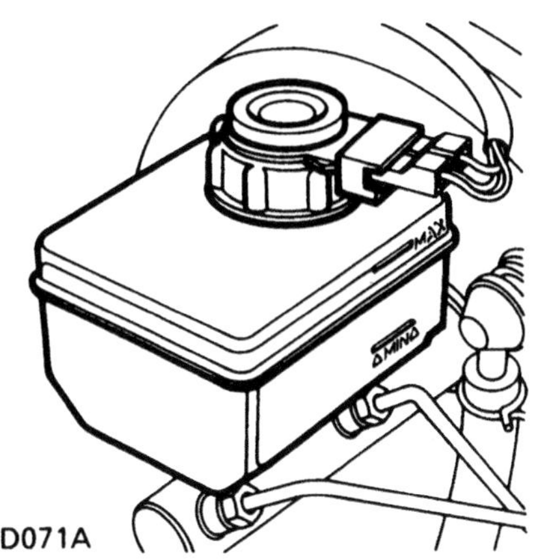

D071A

WARNING

*Contact your dealer immediately if brake
travel is unusually long or if there is any
appreciable drop in brake fluid.*

BRAKE FLUID CHECK

The fluid level will fall slightly during use as a
result of brake pad wear, but should not be
allowed to fall below the 'MIN' mark. Any
substantial drop in fluid indicates a leak in the
system, in which case the vehicle must NOT
be driven and you should contact your dealer.

With the vehicle on level ground, check the
fluid level at least every week (more frequently
in high mileage or arduous operating
conditions). Check the level visually through
the side of the transparent container without
removing the filler cap.

Topping-up

Wipe the filler cap clean before removing to
prevent dirt from entering the reservoir, then
top up to the 'MAX' mark using *FMVSS 116
DOT 4* fluid.

Use only new fluid from an airtight container
(old fluid from opened containers, or fluid
previously bled from the system must NOT be
used).

DO NOT OVERFILL!

WARNING

*DO NOT drive the vehicle with the fluid level
below the 'MIN' mark.*

*Brake fluid will damage painted surfaces;
clean up any spillage immediately and rinse
with plenty of water.*

*If brake fluid should come into contact with
the skin or eyes, rinse immediately with
plenty of water.*

Engine compartment

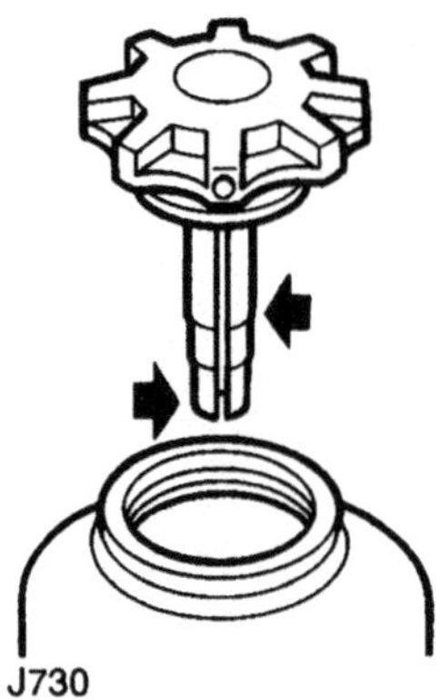

J730

***DO NOT** start the engine if the fluid level has dropped below the dipstick - severe damage to the steering system could result.*

POWER STEERING TOP-UP

ONLY check the fluid level with the engine switched off and the system cold, and ensure that the steering wheel is not turned after stopping the engine.

Wipe the filler cap to prevent dirt from entering the reservoir.

Remove the filler cap and, using a lint-free cloth, wipe the dipstick clean. Refit the cap fully and remove it again to check the fluid level. Ensure the fluid level is between the UPPER mark and the end of the dipstick. If necessary, top up with a fluid meeting *Dexron II D* specification, ensuring no dirt enters the reservoir.

DO NOT fill above the UPPER mark on the dipstick.

Tyres

Never drive your vehicle if the tyres are badly worn, cut or damaged, or if the pressures are incorrect.

Incorrectly inflated tyres wear rapidly and seriously affect the vehicle's safety and road handling characteristics.

Caring for your tyres

Always drive with consideration for the condition of the tyres and frequently inspect the tread and side walls for signs of distortion or damage (in particular, look for lumps, cuts and bulges).

Tyre pressures

Tyre pressures should be checked at least once a week with normal road use, but should be checked DAILY if the vehicle is used off-road.

Check the pressures - including the spare - when the tyres are cold (air pressure naturally increases in warm tyres). The recommended pressures are shown in 'General data'.

If the vehicle has been parked in strong sunlight or is used in high ambient temperatures, DO NOT reduce tyre pressures; instead, move the vehicle into shade and allow the tyres to cool before checking.

Tyre wear

Some tyres fitted as original equipment have wear indicators moulded into the tread pattern. When the tread has worn down to 1.6 mm (1/16 in) the indicators start appearing at the surface of the tread pattern, producing the effect of a continuous band of rubber across the width of the tyre.

A tyre MUST be replaced as soon as an indicator band becomes visible or the tread depth reaches the minimum permitted by legislation.

Tread depth must be checked regularly (at every maintenance service, or more frequently). Always replace a tyre before the tread reaches a remaining depth of 1.6 mm (1/16 in). DO NOT drive with tyres worn to this limit, the safety of the vehicle and its occupants will be adversely affected.

NOTE: After off-road use, check to make sure there are no lumps or bulges in the tyres or exposure of the ply or cord structure.

Valve caps

Keep the valve caps screwed down firmly to prevent dirt from entering the valve.

Replacement tyres

Wheel rims and tyres are matched to suit the handling characteristics of the vehicle. For safety, ALWAYS check that replacement tyres comply with the manufacturer's original specification and that the load rating shown on the side wall is the same as that of the original equipment for a particular territory. Contact your Land Rover dealer for further information or assistance.

Tyres

WARNING

WARNING

ALWAYS use the same make and type of radial-ply tyres front and rear. DO NOT use cross-ply tyres, or interchange tyres from front to rear.

- *If the wheel is marked 'TUBED' an inner tube MUST be fitted, even with a tubeless tyre.*

- *If the wheel is marked 'TUBELESS', an inner tube must NOT be fitted.*

NOTE: *Tyre sizes and pressures are shown in 'General data'.*

WARNING

Do not replace wheels with any type other than genuine Land Rover parts.

Wheels and tyres are designed for both off-road and on-road use and have a very important influence upon the correct operation of the suspension system and vehicle handling.

Alternative wheels which do not meet original equipment specifications should not be fitted.

Snow chains

Land Rover approved snow chains are designed for on-road use in extreme snow conditions only, and are not recommended for off-road use. Always observe the following recommendations:

- ONLY Land Rover approved chains may be fitted to the front wheels, or fitted to all four wheels. Non-approved chains can be fitted to the rear wheels ONLY.

- Ensure the gearbox differential is locked.

- Always adhere to the snow chain fitting and retensioning instructions and the speed limit recommendations for varying road conditions. Never exceed 30 mph (50 km/h).

- Avoid tyre damage by removing snow chains as soon as the road is free of snow.

NOTE: *Snow chains are not available for 265/75 R16 tyres.*

For more information or assistance, consult your Land Rover dealer.

WARNING

DO NOT fit unapproved snow chains to the front wheels - this could damage brake components.

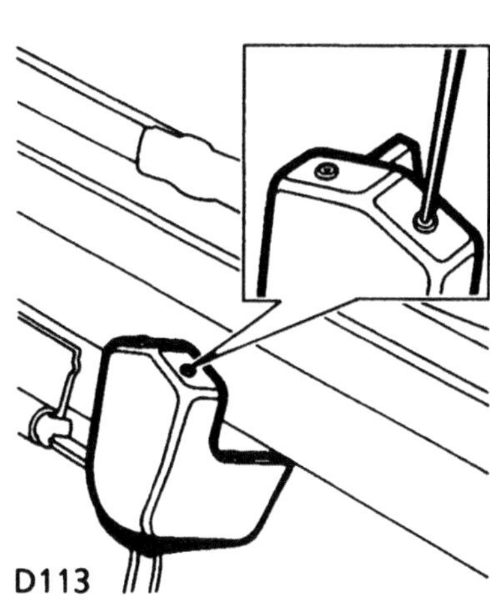

D113

WASHER JETS

To adjust a washer jet, insert a needle into the jet orifice (see inset) and lever gently to position the jet.

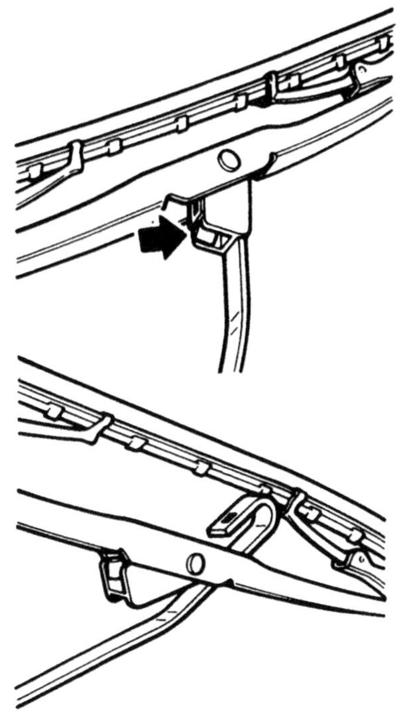

D096

WIPER BLADE REPLACEMENT

To renew a windscreen or rear screen wiper blade, lift the wiper arm away from the windscreen, press the retaining clip (1), push the blade away from the arm and then unhook the wiper blade.

Locate the new blade assembly on the arm, hook it to the swivel bracket and push into engagement until the blade is retained by the clip.

Always fit wiper blades that are identical to the original specification.

Battery

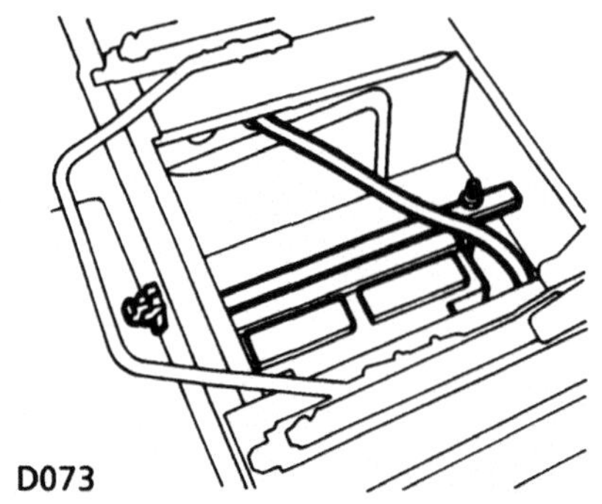

D073

The battery is located underneath the left-hand front seat. Pull up the front of the seat base to release it from its retaining clips and pull it forward. Release the buckle on the front of the battery compartment and slide off the lid.

When refitting the seat base, insert the rear of the base first and then push down firmly to re-engage the retaining clips - ENSURE the seat base is secure before driving.

Batteries contain sulphuric acid. If the acid comes in contact with the eyes or skin, wash immediately with cold water and seek medical advice.

During normal operation batteries emit explosive hydrogen gas - ensure sparks and naked lights are kept away from the battery compartment.

To reduce the risk of a short circuit, remove all metal wrist bands and jewellery before working in the battery compartment and NEVER allow the battery terminals or vehicle leads to make contact with tools or metal parts of the vehicle.

Battery

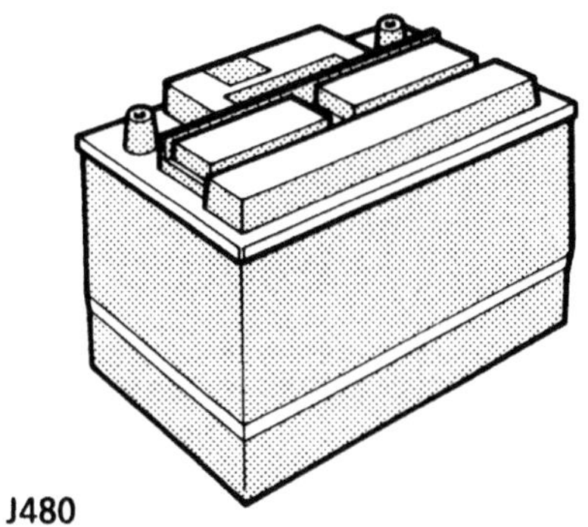

J480

Battery maintenance

The battery fitted to your vehicle requires minimal attention as follows:

- In temperate climates check the electrolyte level once every 3 years. In hot climates check the level annually.

- Occasionally wipe the battery casing to remove dirt and grease.

- Keep the battery terminals clean and free from corrosion by occasionally smearing them with petroleum jelly.

Checking the electrolyte level

Gently prise off the vent covers (or unscrew if vent plugs are fitted) and inspect the electrolyte level of the centre cell. This should be no lower than 1 mm (0.04 in) above the top of the plates. If necessary, top up with distilled water to a maximum of 3 mm (0.12 in) above the plates.

Battery removal and replacement

Your vehicle may be fitted with a battery backed-up sounder, which operates as an anti-theft siren if the main battery is disconnected.

If it is necessary to remove the main vehicle battery, it is ESSENTIAL to adopt the following procedure before disconnecting the terminals in order to prevent the siren from sounding:

1. Turn the starter switch 'on' and then 'off'. Then remove the key.

2. Disconnect the vehicle battery WITHIN 15 SECONDS (if it is not disconnected within 15 seconds, the back-up siren will sound immediately the battery terminals are disconnected).

ALWAYS disconnect the negative ('-') terminal first. When replacing, connect the positive ('+') terminal first.

If the siren sounds when the battery is reconnected, it CANNOT be turned off in the normal way (ie. by operating the handset buttons). To deactivate the siren, disarm the alarm system with the handset and turn the starter switch to position 'II'.

Battery

To avoid damaging the vehicle's electrical system, ensure correct polarity when refitting the battery.

ONLY fit a replacement battery of the same type and specification as the original. Other batteries may vary in size and have different terminal positions, capable of creating a potential fire hazard if the terminals or leads were to come into contact with the battery clamp assembly.

DO NOT use a high speed battery charger as a starting aid.

DO NOT let the engine run without the battery connected.

Cold climates

Where ambient temperatures are consistently below freezing point, a heater should be used to keep the battery warm while the vehicle is not in use. Consult your Land Rover dealer for recommendations.

Battery charging

Batteries generate explosive gases, contain corrosive acid and supply levels of electric current high enough to cause serious burns. Before charging, ensure the battery is properly topped up, and ALWAYS observe the following precautions while charging the battery:

- Always remove the battery from the vehicle.

- Make sure the battery charger is disconnected from its power supply before connecting the leads to the battery terminals.

- Make sure the charging leads are securely clamped before switching on the charger, and DO NOT move the clamps while the charger is switched on.

- Shield your eyes or avoid leaning over the battery.

- Keep the area around the top of the battery well ventilated.

- Keep naked lights clear of the battery (batteries emit inflammable hydrogen during and after charging).

- When charging is complete, switch off the charger before disconnecting the charging leads, and then leave the battery for an hour BEFORE reconnection to the vehicle.

Wheel changing

IMPORTANT INFORMATION
Before jacking the vehicle always observe the following precautions!

- Park your vehicle away from the thoroughfare, and make your passengers wait in a safe area AWAY from the vehicle.

- Switch on the hazard warning lights to alert other road users.

- ALWAYS engage the differential lock before jacking (warning light on fascia illuminates).

- Apply the handbrake and engage 1st gear in the main gear box and select 'L' in the transfer box. Turn off the starter switch and remove the key.

- NEVER jack the vehicle with passengers inside, or with a caravan or trailer connected!

- NEVER work beneath the vehicle with the jack as the only means of support. The jack is designed for wheel changing only!

D074

Using the Wheel Chock

WARNING

Before raising the vehicle, it is ESSENTIAL to chock one of the road wheels; the handbrake acts on the transmission, not on the rear wheels, and therefore may not hold the vehicle when raised.

WARNING

Always chock the wheel diagonally opposite the one to be removed - chocking the front of a front wheel or the back of a rear wheel, using the chock provided.

NOTE: The wheel chock is stowed in a compartment under the left-hand front seat (see 'Battery' for details of access).

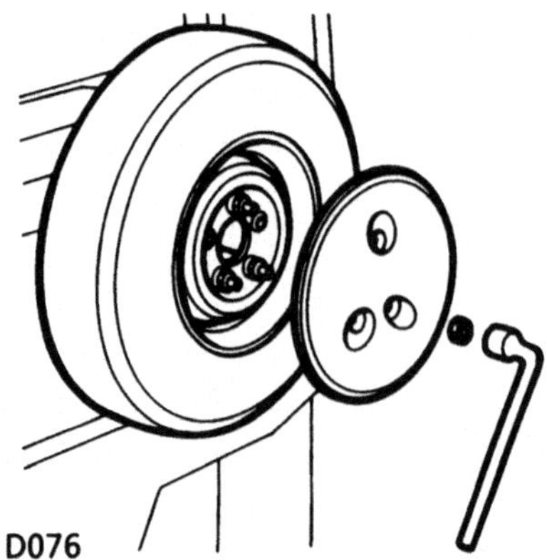

D076

Removing the spare wheel

1. Remove the nuts securing the wheel cover using the wheel brace supplied in the tool kit.

2. Remove the nuts securing the spare wheel to the carrier and lift off the wheel.

WARNING

DO NOT use the spare wheel securing nuts in place of the road wheel nuts.

The wheels are extremely heavy. Take care when lifting and particularly when removing the spare wheel from its mounting position on the bonnet or rear door.

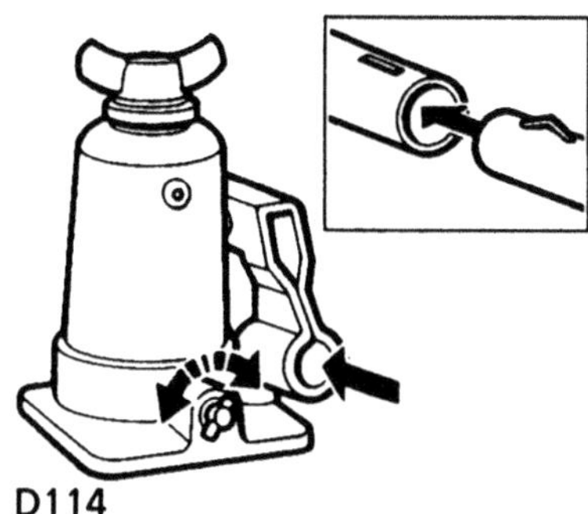

D114

VEHICLE JACKING

One of two types of jack will have been
supplied with your vehicle - either a bottle jack
or pillar jack. The operation of each type
differs greatly and it is important to read the
appropriate operating instructions that follow.

The bottle jack (if fitted) is stowed in a
compartment under the left-hand front seat
(see 'Battery' for details of access). The jack
handle and tools (or pillar jack - if fitted) are
stowed in a bag behind the front seat in
'Pick-up' and 'Hard-top' models and under the
bench seat in 'Soft-top' and 'Station Wagon'
models.

Operating the bottle jack

Slot the jack lever together, ensuring that the
spring clip protrudes from the engagement
slot where the two parts join (see inset). Close
the jack release valve by turning it fully
clockwise and insert the lever into the socket
where shown. Pump the lever up and down to
raise the jack.

To lower the jack, withdraw the lever and slot
the notched end over the the pegs on the
release valve. Slowly turn the release valve
anti-clockwise allowing the weight of the
vehicle to lower the jack.

Wheel changing

Positioning the bottle jack

Always position the jack from the front or rear of the vehicle directly in line with the jacking points.

NEVER use the jack from the side of the vehicle.

Always use the complete, two piece, jack lever throughout to minimise any accidental contact with a hot exhaust system.

ONLY jack the vehicle using the jack location points described or damage to the vehicle could occur.

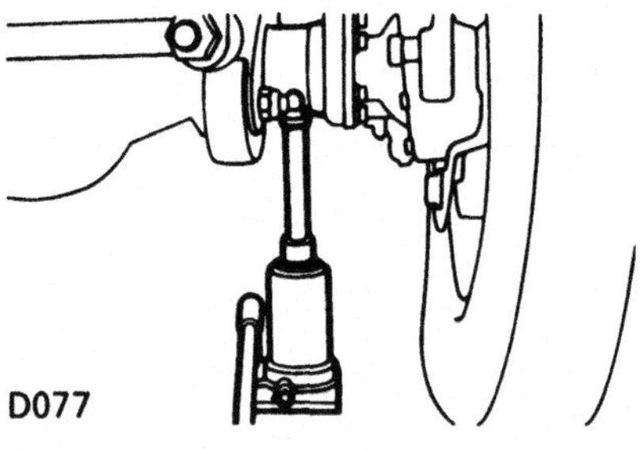

D077

Front jacking point:

Position the jack so that, when raised, it engages with the front axle casing immediately below the coil spring. The jack cradle must locate between the flange at the end of the axle casing and the large bracket to which the front suspension members are mounted.

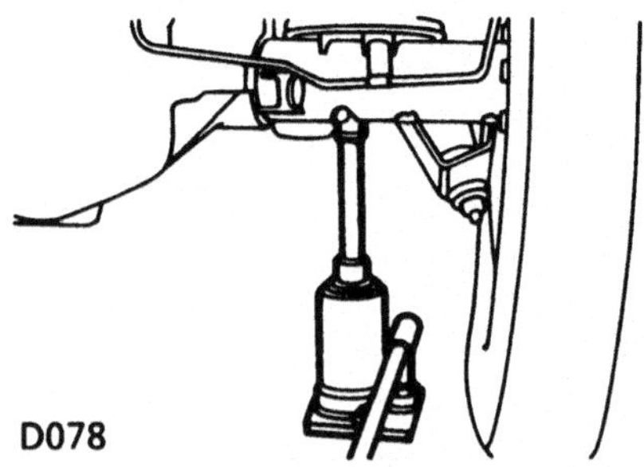

D078

Rear jacking point:

Push the mud flap up over the tyre to allow clear access (return it to its correct position when the wheel change is complete). Position the jack so that, when raised, it engages with the rear axle casing immediately below the coil spring and as close as possible to the shock absorber mounting bracket.

Care of the jack

Occasionally, clean and grease the moving parts (particularly the ram/pillar) to prevent rust.

The bottle jack oil level should be checked at normal servicing intervals and if necessary topped up with an hydraulic oil with a viscosity to BS 4231 grade 32 and ISO proof 32.

To avoid contamination, the bottle jack should always be returned to its fully closed position and must always be stowed upright.

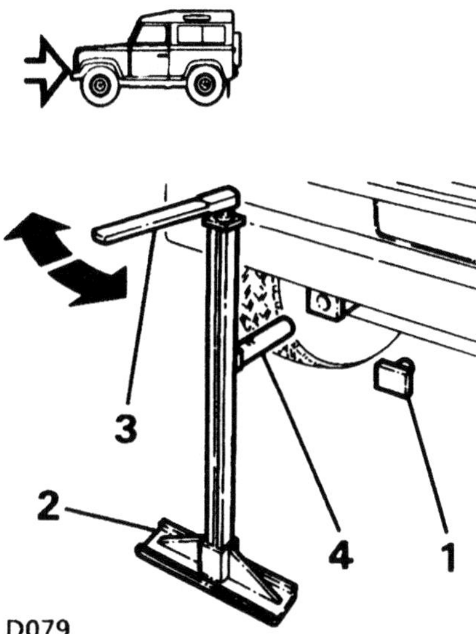

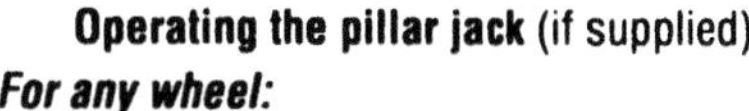

D079

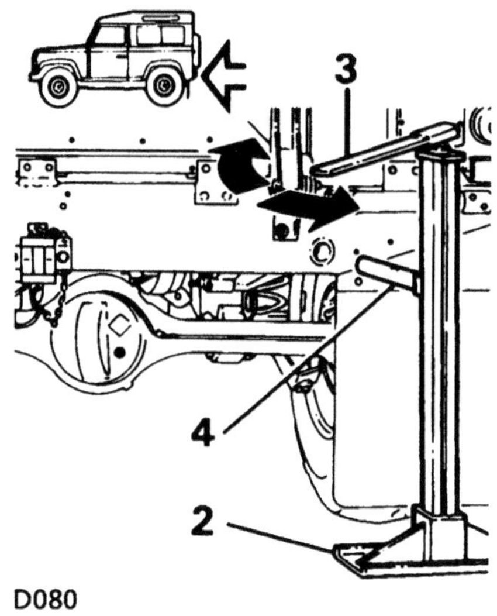

D080

Operating the pillar jack (if supplied)

For any wheel:

1. Remove the rubber plug (1) from the jacking tube corresponding to the wheel to be changed.

2. Insert the jack pillar into the base (2).

3. Fit the handle (3) to the pillar and adjust the height so the jacking peg (4) can be inserted into the jacking tube.

NOTE: The jack handle operates as a ratchet - one side raises the jack, then turn the handle over to lower the jack.

Wheel changing

Changing a wheel

Before raising the vehicle, ensure that all the precautions listed at the beginning of this section have been observed. Also, ensure that the wheel chock is correctly positioned, as described previously.

In some markets, vehicles fitted with alloy wheels have one locking wheel nut fitted to each wheel. Refer to 'Locking wheel nuts' later in this section before changing an alloy wheel.

- Use the wheel brace to slacken the wheel nuts half a turn anti-clockwise.

- Raise the vehicle until the tyre is clear of the ground, and remove the wheel nuts and wheel (DO NOT damage the surface of alloy wheels (if fitted) by placing them face down on the road).

- Lightly oil or grease the wheel studs to assist in wheel replacement, ensuring that no oil or grease comes into contact with the brake components.

- On vehicles fitted with alloy wheels, lightly oil or grease (using an approved anti-seize compound) the wheel mounting spigot to minimise the tendency for adhesion between the wheel and the spigot. Ensure that no oil or compound comes into contact with the brake components. If, due to an emergency situation, this treatment is not practicable; refit the spare wheel for the time being, but remove and treat the wheel at the earliest opportunity.

- Fit the spare wheel and lightly tighten the wheel nuts, ensuring they are firmly seated. DO NOT fully tighten whilst the tyre is clear of the ground.

- Lower the vehicle and remove the jack and wheel chock.

- Fully tighten the wheel nuts. DO NOT OVERTIGHTEN by using foot pressure or extension bars on the wheel brace, as this could overstress the wheel studs.

- REMEMBER to disengage the differential lock and change to 'H' (high range) before driving.

- Finally, check the tyre pressure and wheel nut torque at the earliest opportunity, see 'General data'.

LOCKING WHEEL NUTS

In some markets, vehicles fitted with alloy
wheels are equipped with a locking wheel nut
on each wheel. The locking wheel nut covers
are visually very similar to standard wheel
nuts but can be identified by a concave indent
on the surface. The locking wheel nut and
cover can only be removed using the special
tools provided, as follows:

- Push the extractor tool (1) firmly over the
  stainless steel nut cover (2).

- Pull the extractor tool **squarely** away from
  the wheel to remove the nut cover and
  reveal the locking wheel nut (3).

- Fit the metal key socket (4) securely over
  the locking wheel nut (3).

- Fit the wheel nut wrench onto the key
  socket and unscrew the nut in the normal
  way.

A code letter is stamped on the face of the key
socket. Ensure the code letter is entered in the
space provided on your Security Information
card - you will need to quote this letter if
replacement components are required. Keep
the card in a safe place away from the vehicle.

For security reasons, store the key socket and
extractor tool out of sight, in a secure place in
the vehicle.

*NOTE: If the extractor tool has been
inadvertently pushed onto a standard wheel
nut, it can be removed ONLY by first undoing
and removing the nut; slide the wheel nut
wrench down the centre of the extractor and
onto the wheel nut.*

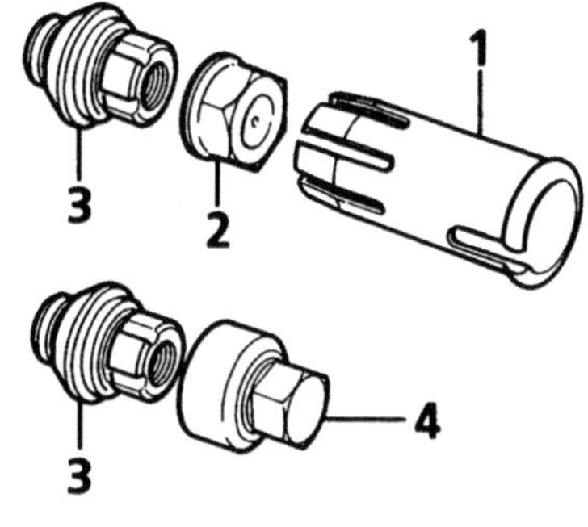

WADING PLUGS

WARNING

For safety, DO NOT work underneath the vehicle unless it is safely parked with the wheels chocked, or is supported by heavy duty stands.

Under severe wading conditions, the timing cover and flywheel housing must be sealed to prevent the ingress of mud and water. Fit the plugs, supplied in the tool kit, as illustrated. Remove the plugs immediately after wading, or periodically if the vehicle is required to do prolonged wading or very muddy work.

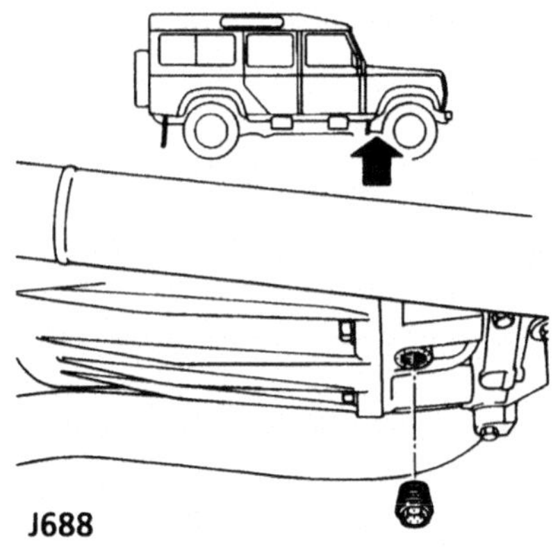

Flywheel housing - 300 TDi

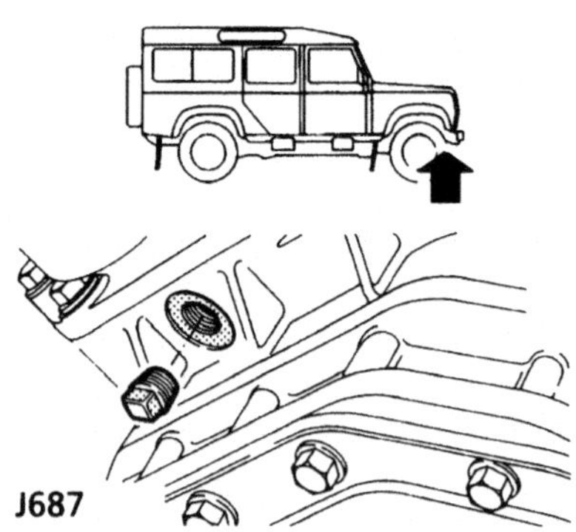

Engine front timing cover - 300 TDi

Fuses

Fuses are simple circuit breakers which protect electrical equipment by preventing the electrical circuits from being overloaded.

Always remove the starter key and switch off the affected circuit before removing a fuse.

Press the fuse extractor (located on the inside of the main fuse box cover) onto the head of the fuse and pull to remove. Fit a new fuse of the same rating. If the replacement fuse fails immediately, contact your local Land Rover dealer and have the circuit checked.

WARNING

Fit only replacement fuses of the same rating and type. Always rectify the cause of a failure before replacing a fuse. Seek qualified assistance if necessary.

Fuses are colour coded to help identify their amperage, as follows:

TAN	5
BROWN	7.5
RED	10
BLUE	15
YELLOW	20
GREEN	30 (air conditioned models only)

The main fuse box is fitted in the centre of the dashboard, in front of the main gear lever. Remove the cover by releasing the fixing screws.

A label in the fuse box cover shows the circuits protected, the fuse ratings and their locations. They are also listed on the following page.

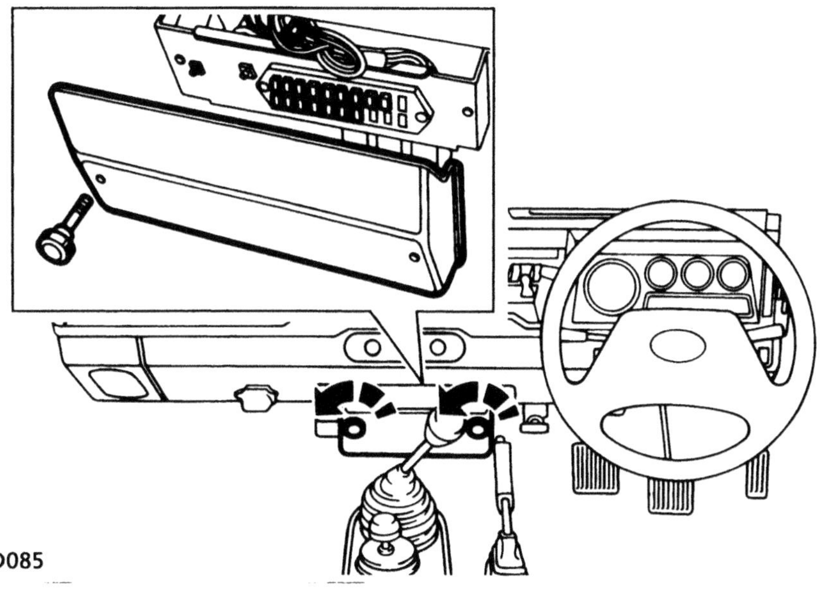

D085

Fuses

MAIN FUSE BOX

Fuse No.	Value (amps)	Electrical circuit
1	15	Hazard warning lights
2	20	Interior light, horn
3	15	Wipers & washers - rear
4	10	Wipers & washers - front
5	15	Heater
6	7.5	Rear fog guard lights
7	5	Radio/cassette player
8	15	Heated rear window
9	10	Cigar lighter
10	20	Alarm sounder
11	7.5	Headlight - RH, dipped beam
12	7.5	Headlight - LH, dipped beam
13	7.5	Headlight - RH, main beam
14	7.5	Headlight - LH, main beam
15	5	Side lights - LH
16	5	Side lights - RH
17	15	Stop & reverse lights
18	20	Air conditioning
19	5	Air conditioning
20	5	Alarm system

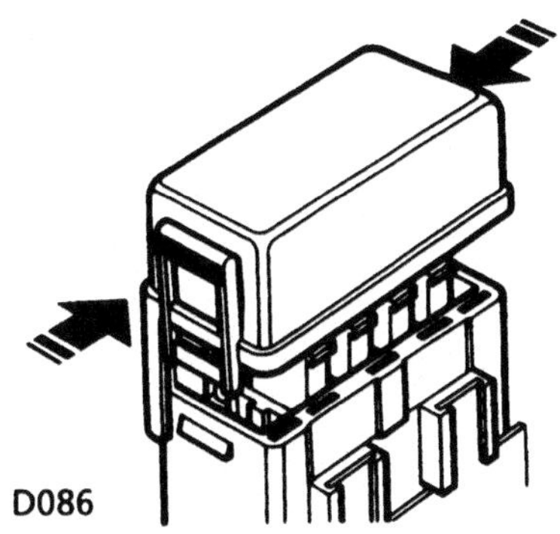

D086

ENGINE COMPARTMENT FUSE BOX

A second fuse box, containing four main fuses is located on the left side of the engine compartment attached to the bulkhead.

The circuits protected, their locations and their ratings will vary from model to model in the vehicle range.

WARNING

Fit only replacement fuses of the same rating and type. Always rectify the cause of a failure before replacing a fuse. Seek qualified assistance if necessary.

REPLACEMENT BULBS	Watts
Headlights	60/55 (Halogen H4)
Front side lights	5
Side repeater lights	5
Stop lights	21
Tail lights	5
Direction indicator lights	21
Number plate lights	4
Reversing lights	21
Rear fog guard lights	21
Interior lights	10

NOTE: *All bulbs must be rated at 12 volts.*

IMPORTANT INFORMATION

Before replacing a bulb, always switch off the starter switch and appropriate lighting switch to prevent any possibility of a short circuit. Only use new bulbs of the same type and with the same specification.

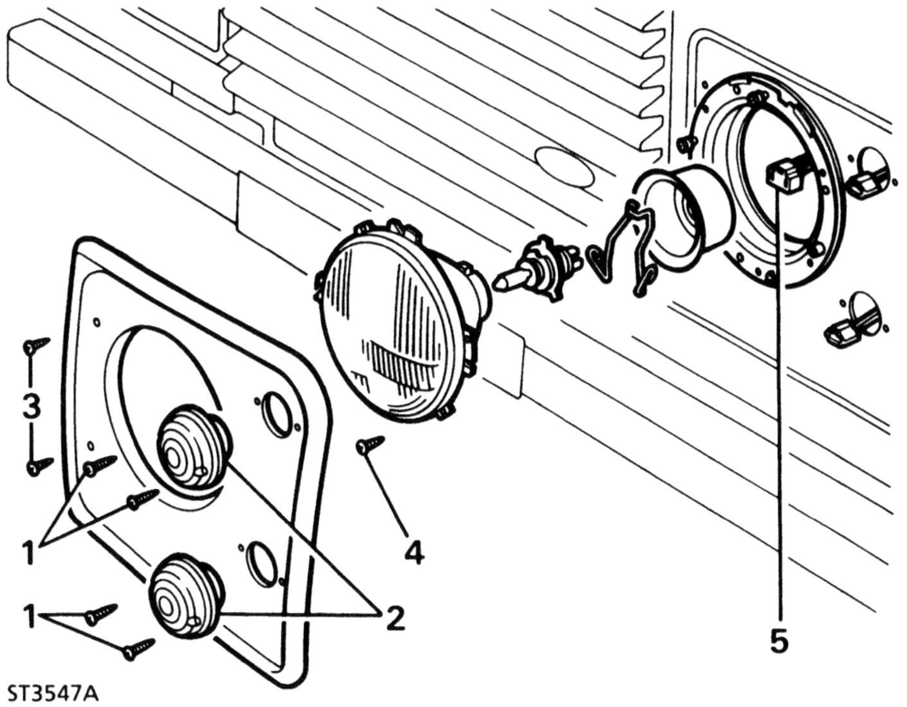

HEADLIGHT UNIT

Light unit removal

To replace the headlight bulb, remove the light
unit as follows:

- Remove the screws (1) retaining the side
  and direction indicator lights (2), release
  them forward and disconnect the plugs.

- Remove the screws (3) and withdraw the
  plastic finisher.

- Remove the headlight retaining screw (4),
  rotate the headlight clockwise to
  disengage and lift out the headlight.

Bulb replacement

Headlight bulb

Disconnect the multi-plug (5) and remove the rubber cover. Unhook the spring clip and withdraw the bulb.

Replace the bulb (the larger of the three tabs uppermost) and secure the spring clip.

Replace the rubber cover, pressing the centre firmly to seal around the electrical contacts of the bulb, then refit the multi-plug.

NOTE: *Do not touch the bulb glass with your fingers. If necessary, clean the bulb with methylated spirits.*

WARNING

ALWAYS fit headlight bulbs and light units with the same Watt value as the original specification (see 'Replacement bulbs'). Fitting a higher rated bulb may result in damage to the 'dim-dip' system.

D087

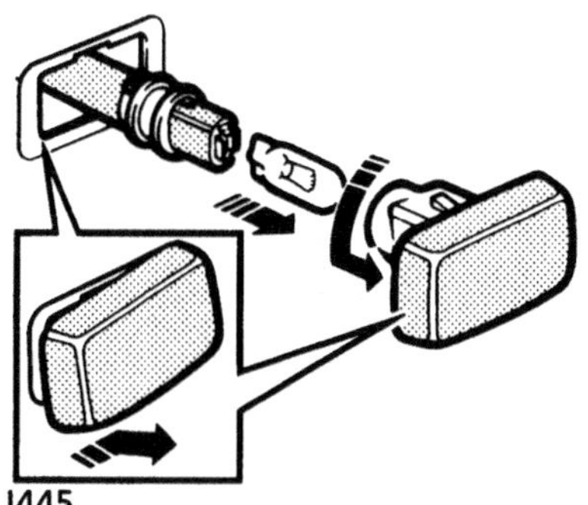

J445

Side, tail, stop and direction indicator bulbs

Remove the retaining screws and withdraw the unit.

Twist the lens anti-clockwise to release the bulb unit.

Push and twist the bulb to remove.

Side repeater light

Push the lens firmly to the right, lift the left edge and withdraw the light unit from the wing.

Twist the bulb holder to release and pull out bulb.

Bulb replacement

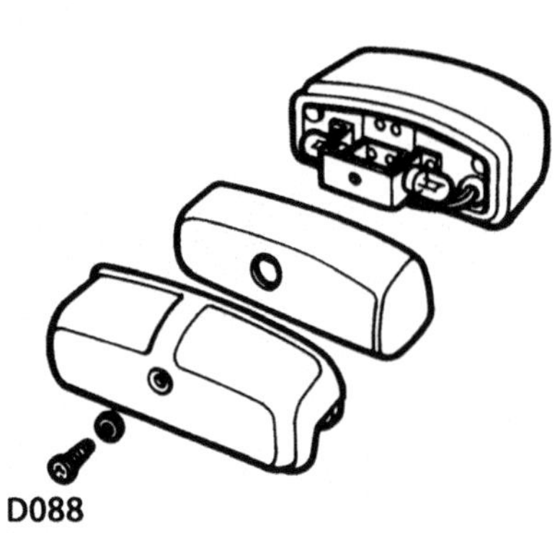

D088

Number plate lights

Remove the securing screw, remove the cover and pull out bulb.

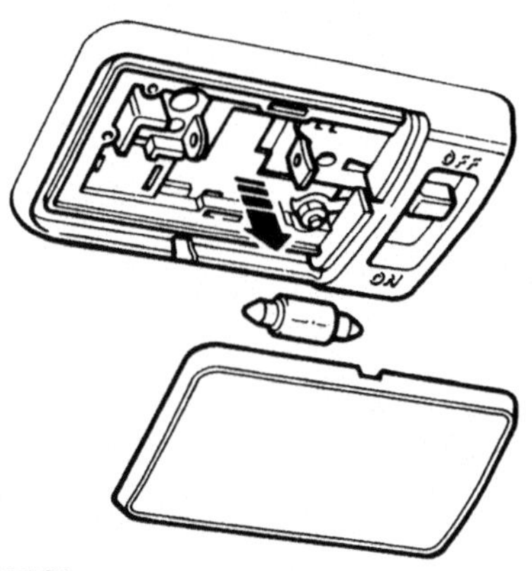

D090

Interior light

Prise the lens from the unit. Spread the bulb holders to release the bulb.

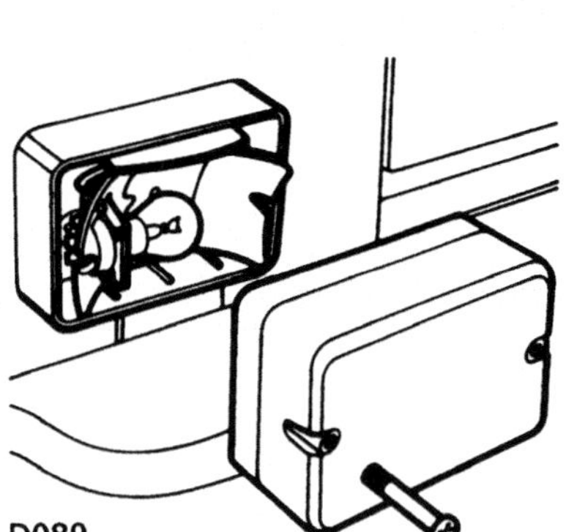

D089

Reverse and rear fog guard lights

Remove the retaining screws and withdraw the lens, then push and twist to release the bulb.

Bulb replacement

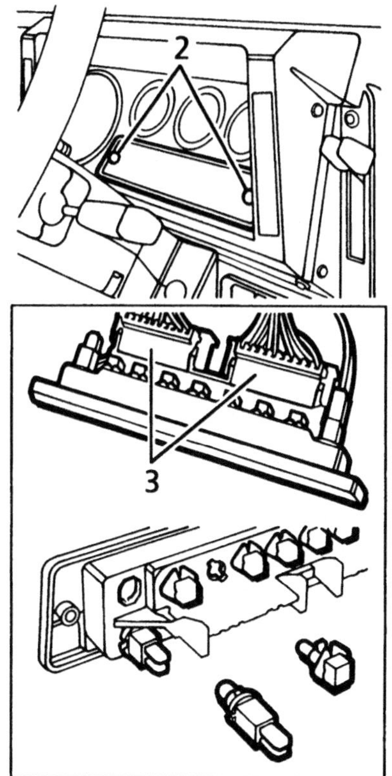

D091

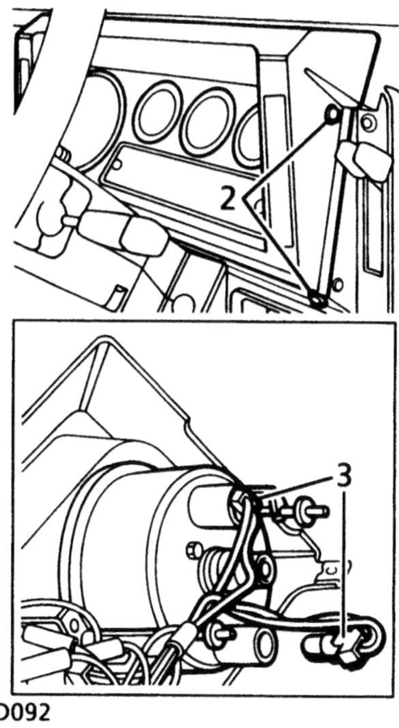

D092

Warning lights

Disconnect the battery (see 'Battery removal and replacement').

Remove the screws (2) and withdraw the warning light module from the instrument panel.

Disconnect the appropriate multi-plug (3), twist and pull out the bulb holder and pull out bulb.

NOTE: Remember to reconnect the battery after replacing a bulb.

Instrument illumination lights

Disconnect the battery (see 'Battery removal and replacement').

Remove the four screws (2) and ease the instrument panel out.

If necessary, the speedometer drive cable can be disconnected to improve access.

Twist and pull out the bulb holder (3) and pull out bulb.

NOTE: Remember to reconnect the battery after replacing a bulb.

Cleaning & vehicle care

WASHING YOUR VEHICLE

Wash your vehicle frequently using a sponge and generous quantities of cold or lukewarm water containing a car shampoo. Rinse and dry off with a chamois leather.

- Do not use hot water!
- Do not use detergent soap products or washing-up liquid!

During winter months when salt has been used on the roads, use a hose to wash the underside of the vehicle. Pay particular attention to wheelarches and panel seams, and to removing accumulations of mud.

Similarly, after off-road driving or wading in muddy or salt water conditions, use a hose to wash underbody components and other exposed parts of the vehicle.

When using a hose, do not direct the jet into the Turbo air intake (if fitted), heater air intake ducts, or through the wheel trim apertures onto the brake components, or at the door, window or sunroof seals, where water pressure could penetrate the seals.

WARNING

Some high pressure cleaning systems are sufficiently powerful to penetrate door or window seals and damage rubbing strips and locking mechanisms. Never aim the water jet directly at components that might easily be damaged.

Steam cleaning

Before steam cleaning the engine compartment, cover the power steering reservoir (if fitted) to prevent contamination. After steam cleaning, ensure that metallic components are carefully rewaxed, especially the steering column, engine water pipes, hose clips and the ignition coil clamp to prevent corrosion.

Getting rid of tar spots

Use white spirit to remove tar spots and stubborn grease stains from paintwork. Then wash immediately to remove all traces of spirit.

Body protection

After washing, inspect the paintwork for damage. Treat paint chips and scratches with touch-up paint to prevent corrosion, and occasionally protect the paint surface with an application of car polish.

Glass & mirrors

Clean the rear window with a soft cloth to avoid damaging the heating elements. DO NOT scrape the glass or use an abrasive cleaning fluid.

Mirror glass is particularly susceptible to damage - DO NOT use abrasive cleaning compounds or metal scrapers.

LOOKING AFTER THE INTERIOR

> **WARNING**
>
> *DO NOT use water to clean the dashboard, damage to the fuses and switches could occur. Instead, clean sparingly with a damp cloth and approved upholstery cleaner.*

- Clean plastic-faced or cloth covered surfaces with diluted upholstery cleaner.

- Steering wheel and trim features should be cleaned with a damp cloth moistened with undiluted upholstery cleaner. Leave for five minutes, and then repeat the operation using a clean cloth and water - but avoid flooding the area! Dry and polish the trim with a dry, lint-free cloth. DO NOT use petrol, detergents, furniture creams or polishes!

- Sweep carpets with a brush or vacuum cleaner and clean with diluted nylon upholstery cleaner.

Clock and radio

- Clean with a dry cloth only! DO NOT use cleaning fluids or sprays.

Seat belts

- Extend belts, then use warm water and a non-detergent soap to clean. Allow to dry naturally, and do not retract until completely dry.

- DO NOT bleach or dye the webbing.

RECOMMENDED CARE PRODUCTS	
(Available in the UK)	
De icer	STC 717
Alloy wheel cleaner	STC 718
Glass cleaner	STC 719
Shampoo	STC 722
Wax polish	STC 723
Screen wash	STC 8249

SECTION 5
Workshop maintenance

WORKSHOP MAINTENANCE

This section covers workshop maintenance for the V8 and Tdi engines only. Maintenance of 4-cylinder petrol and diesel (non-turbo) should be referred to a Land Rover dealer.

It is recommended that the maintenance procedures covered in this section of the handbook, should only be carried out by qualified personnel in a fully equipped workshop; preferably an authorised Land Rover dealer. However, if the vehicle is being operated in a remote area, where full workshop facilities are not available, some maintenance can be carried out, provided that it is completed in safe conditions by experienced personnel.

WARNING

DO NOT carry out any maintenance in dusty, damp or dirty conditions.

NOTE: Some of the servicing procedures require specialised knowledge and equipment, and therefore MUST be carried out by a qualified person, familiar with the maintenance and safety procedures practised by Land Rover dealers. These NECESSARY procedures are NOT covered in this handbook and should be referred to a Land Rover dealer.

Servicing schedules

In normal operating conditions, servicing should be carried out at intervals of 10,000 km (6,000 miles) or every six months, whichever is sooner.

IMPORTANT INFORMATION

Special operating conditions

When a vehicle is operated in extremely arduous conditions, or on dusty, wet or muddy terrain, more frequent attention must be paid to servicing requirements.

For example; if your vehicle experiences deep wading conditions, even DAILY servicing could be necessary to ensure the continued safe and reliable operation of the vehicle.

Contact a Land Rover dealer for advice.

Emission control

Your vehicle is fitted with various items of emission control equipment, designed to meet specific territorial requirements.

You should be aware that unauthorised replacement, modification or tampering with this equipment by an owner or motor vehicle repairer, may be unlawful and subject to legal penalties.

In addition, engine settings must NOT be tampered with. These have been established to ensure that your vehicle complies with stringent exhaust emission regulations. Incorrect engine settings may adversely affect exhaust emissions, engine performance and fuel consumption, as well as causing high temperatures, which will result in damage to the catalytic converter (if fitted) and the vehicle.

Replacement parts

It is essential that only Land Rover parts are used, safety features embodied in the vehicle may be impaired if other, non-approved parts are used. In certain territories, legislation prohibits the fitting of parts not to the manufacturer's specification.

WARNING

The fitting of parts of inferior quality, or the carrying out of non-approved alterations or conversions, may be dangerous and could affect the safety of the vehicle and occupants. It could also invalidate the terms and conditions of the vehicle warranty.

Road testing on dynamometers ('rolling roads')

WARNING

Because your vehicle is equipped with permanent four-wheel drive, it is essential that any dynamometer testing is carried out ONLY by a qualified person, familiar with the dynamometer testing and safety procedures practised by Land Rover dealers. Contact your Land Rover dealer for further information.

SAFETY IN THE GARAGE

Whenever you carry out maintenance on your vehicle, the following safety precautions should be observed at all times.

- ALWAYS keep hands, tools and items of clothing clear of all drive belts and pulleys whilst they are in operation.

- DO NOT touch exhaust or cooling system components until they are cool.

- DO NOT touch electrical leads or components with the starter switch turned on.

- NEVER leave the engine running in an unventilated area; exhaust gases are poisonous and contain carbon monoxide, which can cause unconsciousness and can be fatal.

- DO NOT work beneath the vehicle with the lifting jack as the only means of support.

- Ensure sparks and naked lights are kept away from the engine and battery compartments.

- DO NOT use any lubricants, solvents or sealants etc, without first reading any warnings and instructions supplied with these substances; they could be harmful if improperly used.

WARNING

Remember, cooling fans and air conditioning system condenser fans (if fitted), may continue to operate after the engine is switched off. Always wait until the fans have completely stopped moving before working in the engine compartment.

Fuel system safety

Fuel vapour is highly flammable and in confined spaces, is also very explosive and toxic. When fuel evaporates, it produces 150 times its own volume in vapour and when mixed with air, becomes an easily ignitable mixture; consequently even a small spillage is very dangerous.

It is recommended that you always have a FOAM, CO_2 GAS, or POWDER type fire extinguisher close at hand when working with fuel or the fuel system.

ALWAYS disconnect the battery negative lead BEFORE carrying out work on the fuel system.

WARNING

It is imperative that the battery is disconnected BEFORE and not during any work on the fuel system, as arcing at the battery terminal could ignite fuel vapour in the atmosphere.

Whenever fuel is being handled, transferred or stored, or when carrying out work on the fuel system, all forms of ignition MUST be extinguished or removed, any lighting being used MUST be flameproof and kept clear of the fuel.

Poisonous liquids

Most liquids and lubricants used in motor vehicles are poisonous and should not be consumed or brought into contact with open wounds. These include; battery acid, anti-freeze, brake, clutch and power steering fluid, as well as petrol, diesel, engine oil and windscreen washer additives.

For your own safety, ALWAYS read and obey all instructions printed on labels and containers.

Used engine oil

Prolonged contact with engine oil can cause serious skin disorders, including dermatitis and skin cancer. ALWAYS wash thoroughly after contact.

It is illegal to pollute drains, water courses or soil with toxic chemicals such as used engine oil. ALWAYS dispose of vehicle liquids and lubricants at authorised waste disposal sites, or at garages which provide facilities for the receipt of used engine oil and toxic chemicals. If in doubt, contact your Local Authority for advice.

PROTECT THE ENVIRONMENT!

ENGINE OIL RENEWAL (all engines)

NOTE: For engine oil check & top-up see 'Owner maintenance'.

DO NOT attempt to drain the engine sump if the engine has been running for some time, the engine oil will be hot and may cause severe scalding.

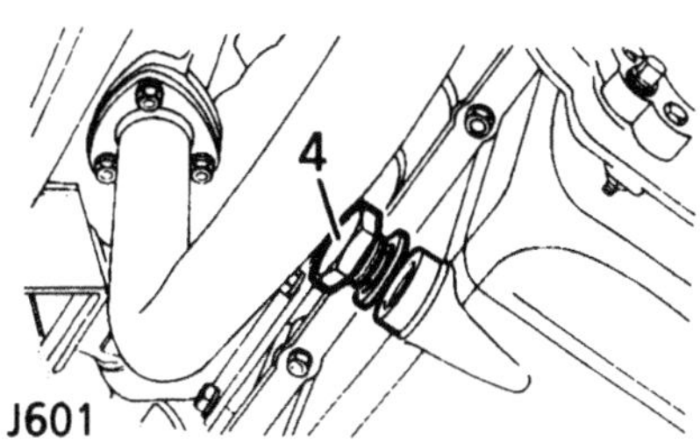

V8 engine

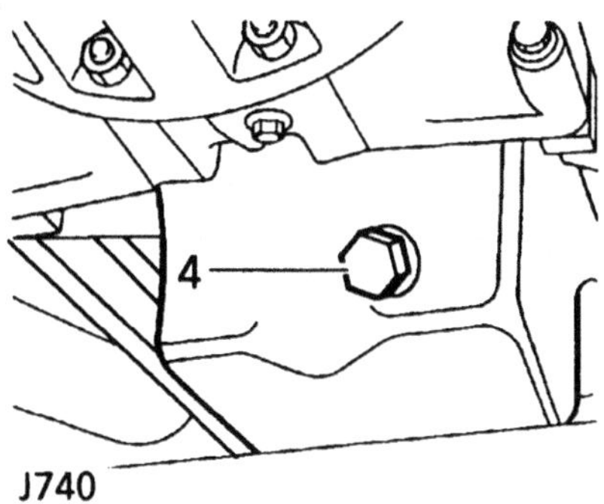

Tdi engine

With the vehicle resting on firm, level ground, run the engine for a few minutes so that the oil will drain more easily. Turn the starter switch to position '0' and disconnect the battery negative lead.

Remove the oil filler cap and position a suitable container under the oil drain plug (4) to collect the used oil.

Remove the drain plug and its washer and allow the oil to drain completely.

NOTE: If, by necessity, this procedure is being carried out in dusty or sandy conditions, refit the drain plug as soon as the main bulk of the oil has drained.

When the sump has fully drained, clean the draining plug and the surrounding area of the sump and refit with a new copper washer.

Refill the sump with fresh oil of the correct specification (see 'General data'). Refit the filler cap and let the vehicle stand for five minutes to allow the oil to drain back into the sump. Check the oil level using the dipstick (as described in 'Owner maintenance') and top up until the correct level is obtained.

- **DO NOT use oil previously drained from the engine.**
- **DO NOT OVERFILL!**

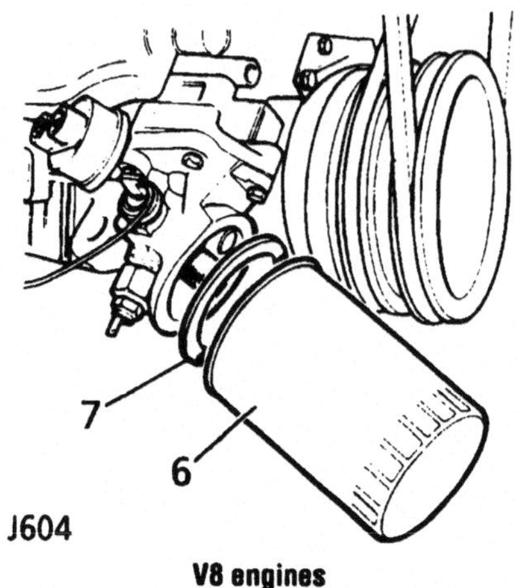

J604

V8 engines

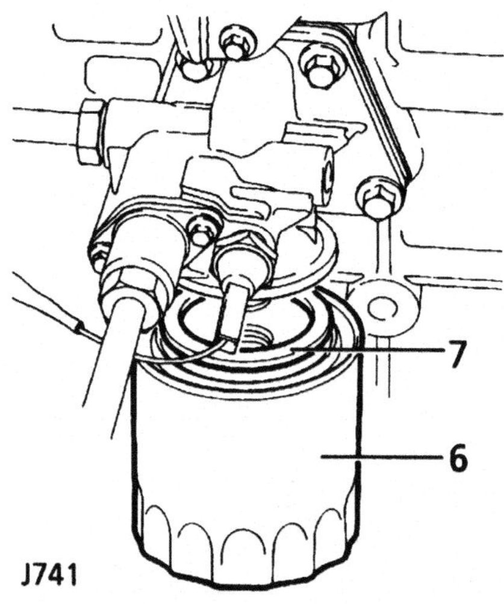

J741

Tdi engines

ENGINE OIL FILTER RENEWAL

To prevent any possibility of air locks in the oil pump, it is recommended that filter renewal is carried out AFTER the engine oil has been changed.

NOTE: *On V8 engines, to minimise the risk of draining the oil pump, ensure that the oil is at the correct operating level before removing the filter.*

- Turn the starter switch to position '0' and disconnect the battery negative lead.

- Clean the area around the head of the filter.

- Place a suitable container beneath the filter.

- Using a strap wrench, unscrew the filter (6) and discard it safely.

- Half fill the filter and smear the rubber washer (7) of the new filter, with clean engine oil of the correct specification (see 'General data').

- Screw the filter on clockwise until the rubber washer touches up against the machined face, then tighten a further half turn using hand pressure only. DO NOT OVERTIGHTEN.

- Connect the battery negative lead and run the engine at a fast idle for five minutes.

- Check the filter for leaks.

Stop the engine and let the vehicle stand for five minutes to let the oil drain back into the sump. Check the oil level (see 'Owner maintenance') and top up if necessary.

FUEL FILTER RENEWAL

Petrol engines

Before carrying out any work on the fuel system, it is essential that you have read and understood the precautions listed at the beginning of the section (see 'Fuel system safety').

The fuel filter is located next to the fuel pump on the right hand side of the chassis (when viewed from the rear).

- Turn the starter switch to position '0' and disconnect the battery negative lead.

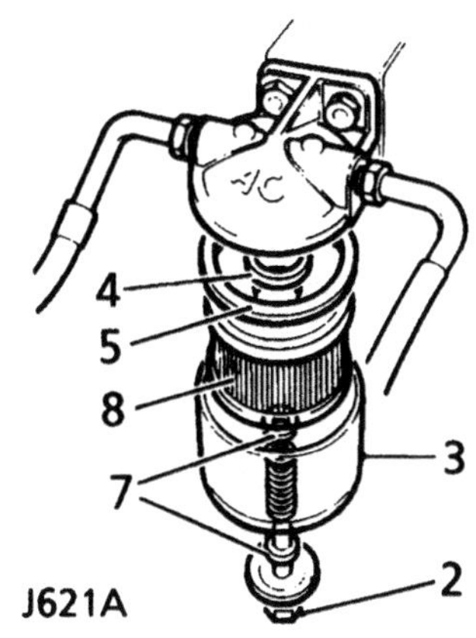

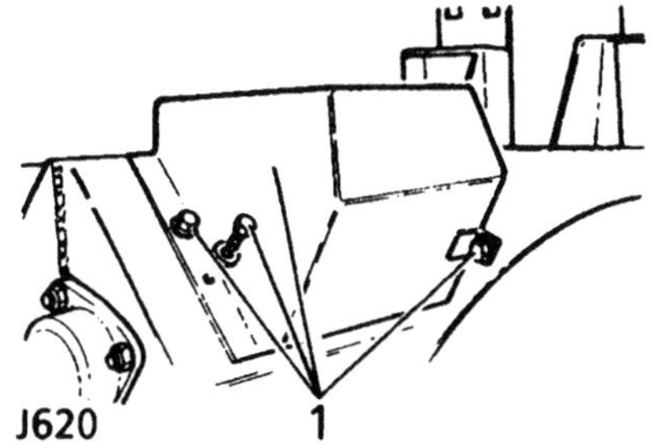

NOTE: *On 110 models the fuel filter is located behind a protective cover (as illustrated above). To remove the cover, unscrew the three bolts (1).*

- Unscrew the centre bolt (2) and withdraw the filter bowl (3).

- Remove the small sealing ring (4) and withdraw the element (8).

- Remove the large sealing ring (5) and discard the old element.

- Clean the filter bowl with clean fuel, ensure the centre and top sealing rings (7) are in good condition. Replace if necessary.

- Fit the new element (small hole downwards) and refit the small and large sealing rings (4 and 5).

- Replace filter bowl and tighten the centre bolt.

- Connect the battery negative lead.

- Start the engine and check for leaks.

Tdi engine

- Turn the starter switch to position '0' and disconnect the battery negative lead.

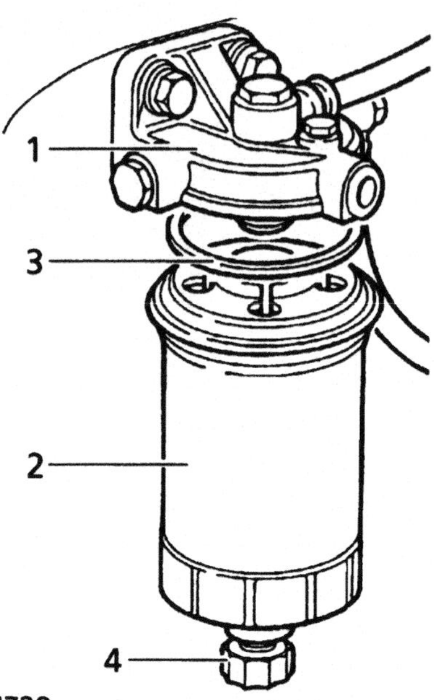

J738

- Clean the area around the filter head (1) and place a container under the filter.

- Using a strap wrench, unscrew the filter (2) and catch the fuel released in the container.

- Wet the seal of the new filter (3) with diesel fuel and screw the filter into position and tighten.

- Ensure that the drain tap (4) at the base of the filter is closed.

- Connect the battery negative lead.

- Start the engine and check for leaks.

FUEL SEDIMENTER CLEANING
(diesel engines - if fitted)

NOTE: *The fuel sedimenter should be drained before removal; this process is covered in 'Owner maintenance'.*

The fuel sedimenter is mounted on the chassis rear side member, near the rear wheel.

- Turn the starter switch to position '0' and disconnect the battery negative lead.

- Fit new seals (4) and re-assemble the sedimenter unit.

- Slacken off the drain plug (5) until pure diesel is emitted, then re-tighten.

- If necessary, prime the system.

- Connect the battery negative lead.

- Start the engine and check the sedimenter for leaks.

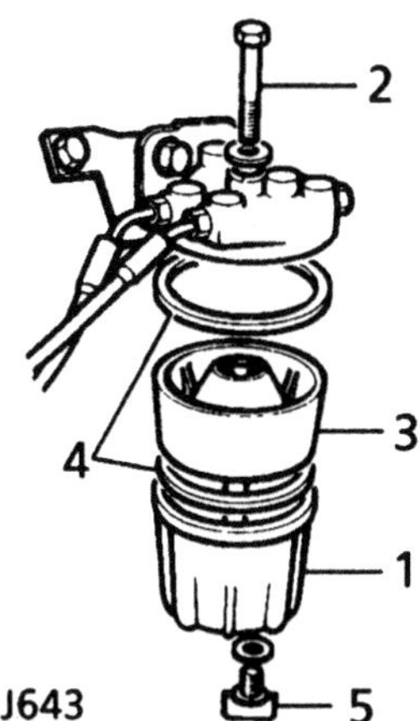

- Disconnect the fuel inlet pipe from the sedimenter and raise the pipe above the level of the fuel tank. The pipe must be kept at this level to prevent the tank from draining.

- Whilst supporting the sedimenter bowl (1), unscrew the bolt on the top of the unit (2) and then remove the bowl.

- Remove the sedimenter element (3) and clean all parts with kerosene.

AIR CLEANER ELEMENT RENEWAL

V8 engine

Engine performance will be seriously affected if the air cleaner element becomes choked with dust and other airborne particles.

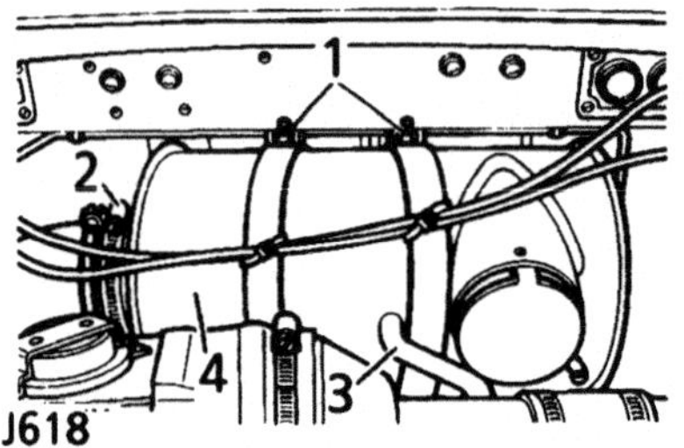

J618

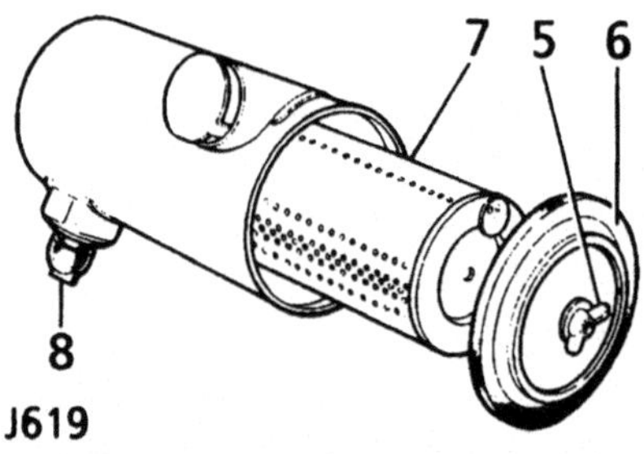

J619

- Unscrew the two retaining nuts (1).

- Disconnect the air cleaner hose (2).

- Remove the engine breather hose (3).

- Withdraw the air cleaner canister (4).

- Unscrew the wing nut and washer (5).

- Remove the filter seal (6).

- Remove the element (7) from the canister.

- Discard the old element, DO NOT attempt to clean it.

- Insert the new element and secure with the wing nut and washer.

- Fit the air cleaner canister.

- Fit the breather hose.

- Fit the air cleaner hose.

- Secure with the retaining straps and nuts.

NOTE: *Check the dump valve (8) (see 'Air cleaner dump valve check').*

Tdi engine

Engine performance will be seriously affected if the air cleaner element becomes choked with dust and other airborne particles.

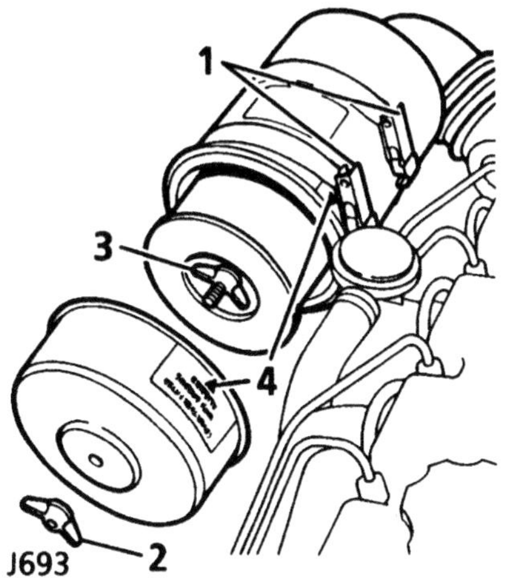

- Release the two retaining clips (1).

- Raise the air cleaner slightly from its cradle to improve access to the element.

- Unscrew the wing nut (2) and remove the end cover.

- Unscrew the wing nut (3) and withdraw the element.

- Clean the interior and exterior of the casing and cover.

- Fit a new element, seal first, into the casing.

- Secure the element with the wing nut.

- Fit the end cover and align the two arrows (4).

- Position the air cleaner in its mounting cradle and secure the two clips (1).

Air cleaner dump valve check - all engines

The dump valve (8) is situated on the
underside of the element housing.

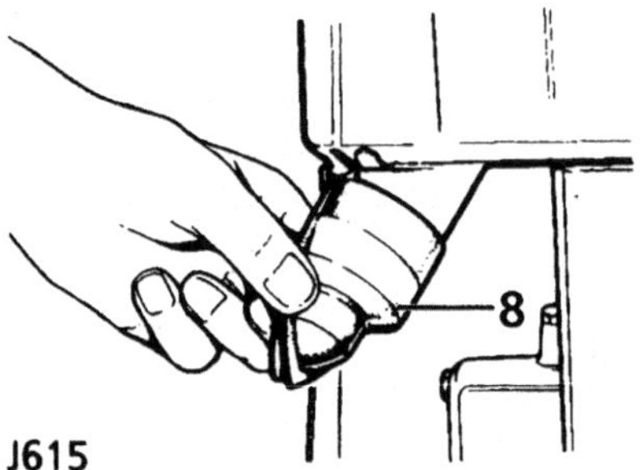

- Squeeze open the dump valve (as
  illustration) and check that the interior is
  clean. Renew the valve if perished.

SPARK PLUG CHECK/RENEWAL
(petrol engines)

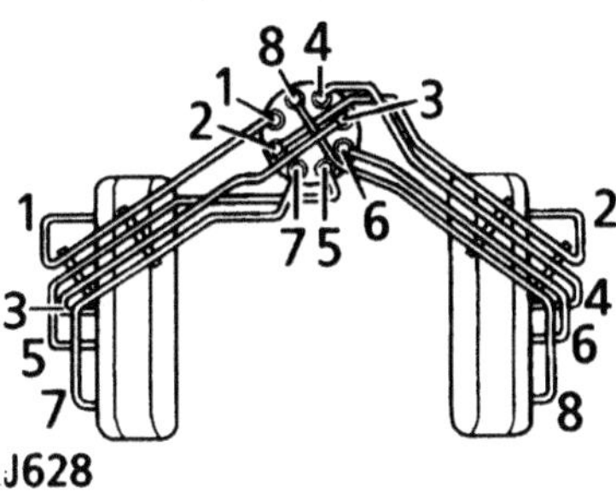

V8 engine

- Remove the HT leads from the spark plugs.

- Remove the plugs using a spark plug socket and ratchet.

- If they are in poor condition, replace with new plugs of the correct specification (see 'General data').

- Set the spark plug gaps to the correct setting (see 'General data').

- Fit the spark plugs and washers - DO NOT OVERTIGHTEN.

NOTE: *Fitting incorrect grades of spark plug, may lead to piston overheating and engine failure.*

- Refit the HT leads in the correct order (as illustration), ensuring that the leads are firmly seated onto the plugs.

IGNITION WIRING & HT LEAD CHECK

Check the HT leads for insulation cracking, or corrosion at end contacts. If the HT leads are damaged, replace with new leads of the same specification.

NOTE: *Ensure leads are reconnected in the correct order or the engine will misfire.*

DISTRIBUTOR

V8 engines

WARNING

ALWAYS disconnect the battery negative lead before carrying out any maintenance on the ignition and electrical systems.

The internal operating parts of the distributor are protected by a plastic insulating cover (1) and are pre-set during manufacture - they do not require maintenance.

WARNING

DO NOT remove or tamper with the plastic insulating cover.

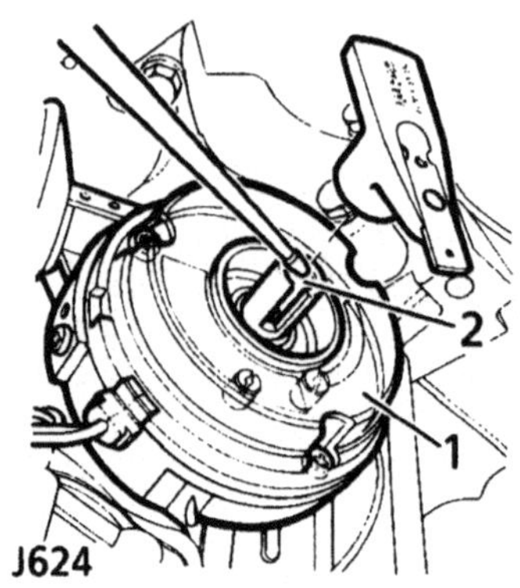

- Clean the outer surfaces of the distributor cap to remove dirt or grease.

- Unclip the cap and check it for cracks. Clean the inside of the cap with a dry, lint free cloth.

- Remove the rotor arm and check it for wear - replace if necessary.

- Apply a spot of clean engine oil to the top of the rotor spindle (2).

- Fit the rotor arm and distributor cap, ensuring that they are properly located. Secure the distributor cap with the two clips.

DRIVE BELTS

Driving belt tension

All pulleys and belts should be examined regularly for any damage, deterioration or fouling (grit, mud, oil etc). Replace or clean where necessary.

After every off-road session, the drive belts should be inspected for cuts and possible damage caused by stones. If a belt has jumped, reposition it correctly and, if necessary, replace it at the earliest opportunity.

WARNING

Before checking or adjusting any drive belt; to prevent the possibility of serious injury, disconnect the battery negative lead to prevent the engine from being started.

DRIVE BELT - 300 Tdi engine

The 300 Tdi engine uses a 'serpentine' type drive belt, which drives all the ancillaries except for the air conditioning compressor and 24 Volt alternator (if fitted).

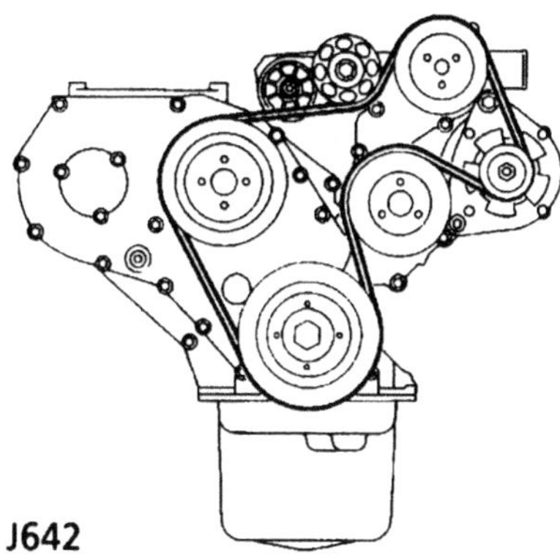

J642

An automatic drive belt tensioner keeps the belt at the correct tension, thereby eliminating the need to manually check the belt deflection.

Under normal highway use, the belt must be changed at 160,000 km (96,000 mile) or eight year intervals (whichever occurs first), but should be examined regularly for signs of wear, splitting or oil contamination and replaced accordingly.

ALTERNATOR DRIVE BELT

V8 engine (without air-conditioning)

Check the belt deflection with thumb pressure, mid-way between the alternator and crankshaft pulleys. Movement should be approximately 12 mm (0.5 in). If adjustment is necessary;

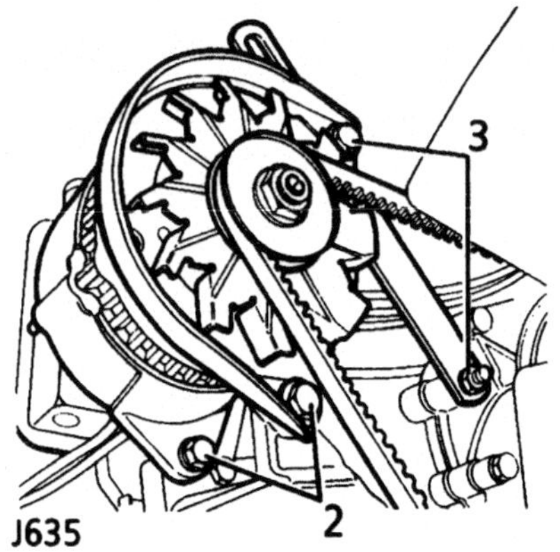

V8 engine (with air-conditioning)

Check the belt deflection with thumb pressure, mid-way between the steering pump and alternator pulleys (arrowed (1) in illustration). Movement should be between 4 and 6 mm (0.16 and 0.25 in). If adjustment is necessary;

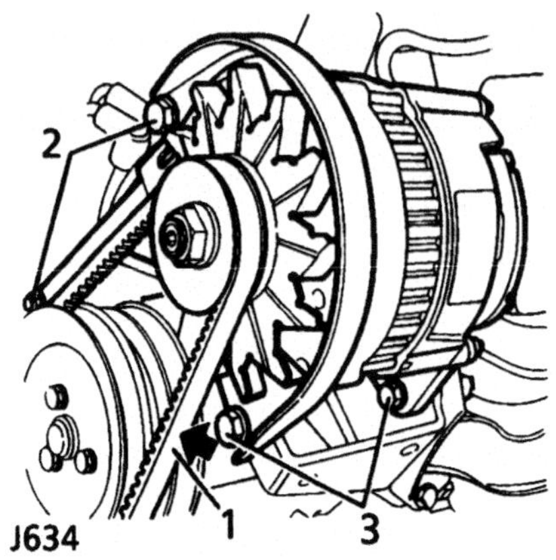

- Turn the starter switch to position '0' and disconnect the battery negative lead.

- Loosen bolts (2).

- Loosen the adjustment bolts (3).

- Pivot the alternator away from, or towards the engine, to increase, or reduce tension.

- Tighten the UPPER adjustment bolt (3).

- Tighten the LOWER adjustment bolt (3).

- Tighten both bolts (2).

- Connect the battery, run the engine for five minutes at a fast idle and then switch off.

- Re-check belt tension.

- Turn the starter switch to position '0' and disconnect the battery negative lead.

- Slacken the adjustment link clamp and pivot bolts (2).

- Slacken the two alternator pivot bolts (3).

- Move the alternator towards, or away from the engine to decrease, or increase tension.

- Tighten the adjustment link clamp and pivot bolts (2).

- Tighten the alternator pivot bolts (3).

- Connect the battery, run the engine for five minutes at a fast idle and then switch off.

- Re-check belt tension.

POWER STEERING PUMP DRIVE BELT

V8 engine
(without air-conditioning)

Check belt deflection with thumb pressure mid-way between the crankshaft and steering pump pulley. Movement should be between 4 and 6 mm (0.16 and 0.25 in). If adjustment is necessary;

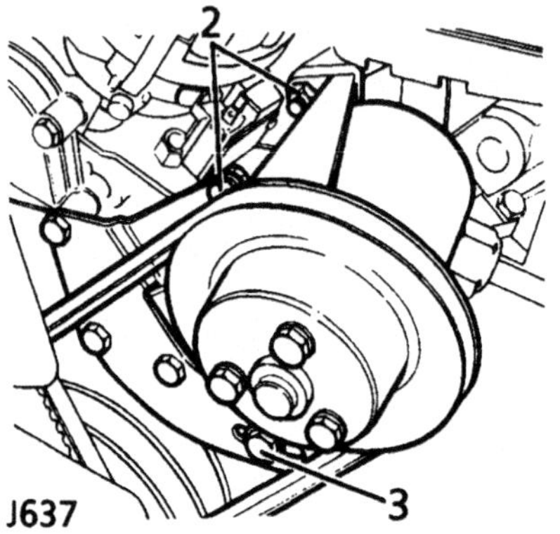

- Turn the starter switch to position '0' and disconnect the battery negative lead.

- Slacken the two pivot bolts (2).

- Slacken the pump adjustment clamp bolt (3).

- Move the pump in the required direction to obtain the correct tension.

DO NOT lever, or apply pressure to the pump body to tension the belt, as damage to the pump may occur.

- Tighten adjustment clamp bolt (3).

- Tighten the two pivot bolts (2).

- Connect the battery, run the engine for five minutes at a fast idle and then switch off.

- Re-check belt tension.

POWER STEERING PUMP DRIVE BELT

V8 engine
(with air-conditioning)

Check the belt deflection with thumb pressure, mid-way between the crankshaft and steering pump pulleys. Movement should be between 4 and 6 mm (0.16 and 0.25 in). If adjustment is necessary;

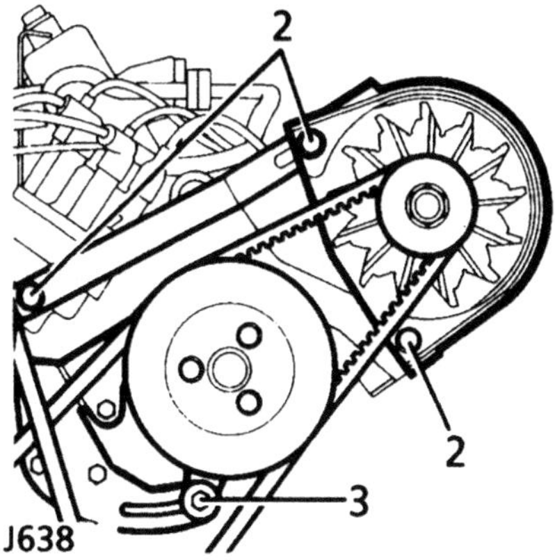

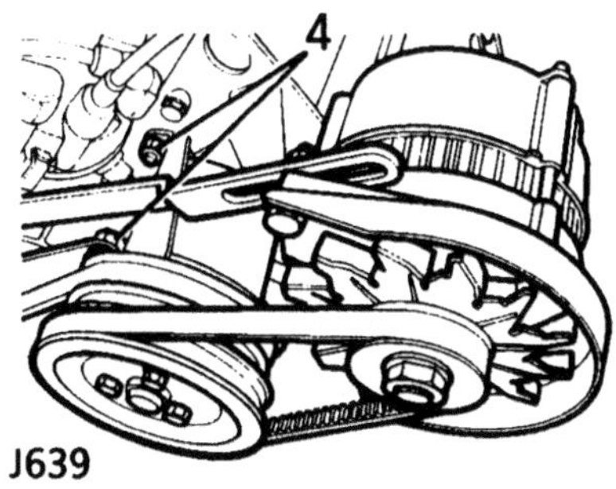

- Slacken the two steering pump pivot bolts (4).

- Move the steering pump in the required direction to achieve the correct tension.

DO NOT lever, or apply pressure to the pump body to tension the belt, as damage to the pump may occur.

- Turn the starter switch to position '0' and disconnect the battery negative lead.

- Slacken the alternator adjustment link clamp and pivot bolts (2) (see 'Alternator drive belt - V8 engine with air-conditioning').

- Slacken the steering pump adjustment clamp bolt (3).

- Tighten the pump adjustment clamp bolt (3).

- Tighten the two pump pivot bolts (4).

- Adjust the alternator drive belt (see 'Alternator drive belt - V8 engine with air-conditioning').

- Connect the battery, run the engine for five minutes at a fast idle and then switch off.

- Re-check both steering pump and alternator belt tension.

AIR CONDITIONING COMPRESSOR
DRIVE BELT

Tdi engine

Correct belt tension an only be achieved using
a suitably calibrated torque meter.

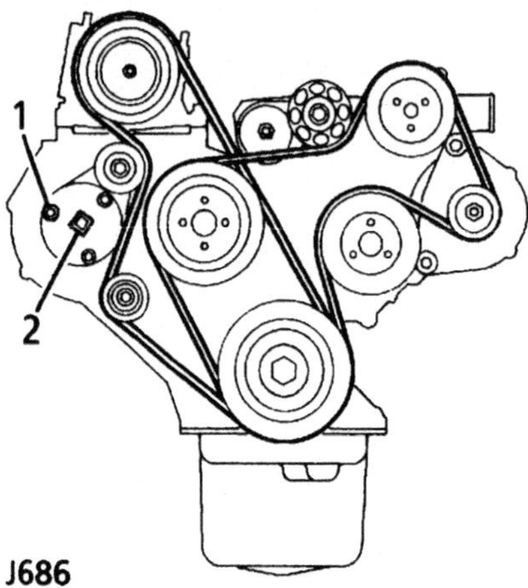

J686

- Slacken the 3 bolts (1) securing the
  tensioner.

- Apply a clockwise torque of 35 Nm to the
  square drive (2) of the tensioner and
  tighten the bolts to 25 Nm.

AIR CONDITIONING COMPRESSOR DRIVE BELT

V8 engine

Check the belt deflection with thumb pressure, mid-way between the compressor and fan/water pump pulley. Movement should be approximately 4 mm to 6 mm (0.16 to 0.25 in). If adjustment is necessary;

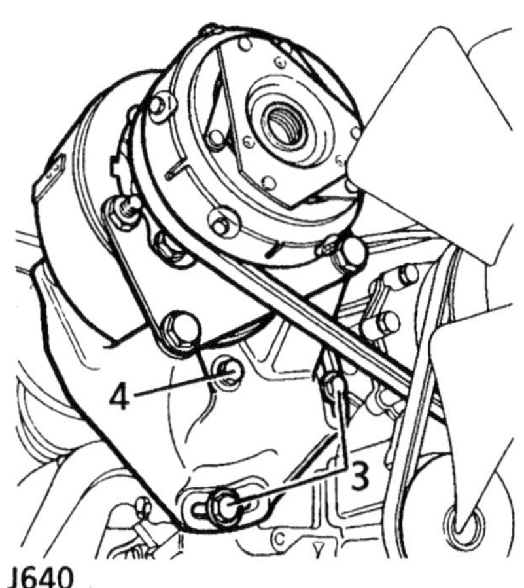

J640

- Turn the starter switch to position '0' and disconnect the battery negative lead.

- Slacken the two compressor mounting bracket clamp bolts (3).

- Slacken the pivot bolt (4) in the centre of the bracket.

- Move the compressor towards/away from the engine, to decrease/increase the tension as required.

DO NOT lever, or apply pressure to the compressor, as this could cause permanent damage.

- Tighten the clamp bolts (3).

- Tighten the pivot bolt (4).

- Check tension.

- Connect the battery, run the engine for five minutes at a fast idle and then switch off.

- Re-check the belt tension.

FAN BELT

V8 engine (with air conditioning)

On vehicles fitted with air conditioning, a tensioner pulley is fitted. Check the belt deflection with thumb pressure, mid-way between the fan and crankshaft pulleys, on the side opposite the tensioner pulley. Movement should be approximately 4 mm to 6 mm (0.16 to 0.25 in). If adjustment is necessary;

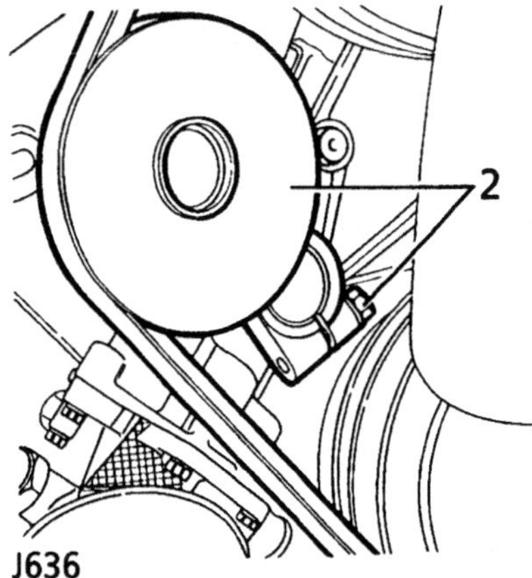

J636

- Turn the starter switch to position '0' and disconnect the battery negative lead.

- Slacken the tensioner pulley pinch bolt (2).

- Move the pulley to the left/right to increase/decrease tension.

- Tighten the pulley pinch bolt.

- Connect the battery, run the engine for five minutes at a fast idle and then switch off.

- Re-check the belt tension.

MAIN GEARBOX OIL RENEWAL

WARNING

For safety, DO NOT work underneath the vehicle unless it is safely parked with the wheels chocked, or is supported by heavy duty stands.

Extreme care should be taken when draining gearbox oil, it may be hot and cause severe scalding.

Ensure the vehicle is parked on firm, level ground and chock the wheels. Place a suitable container under the gearbox to catch the used oil.

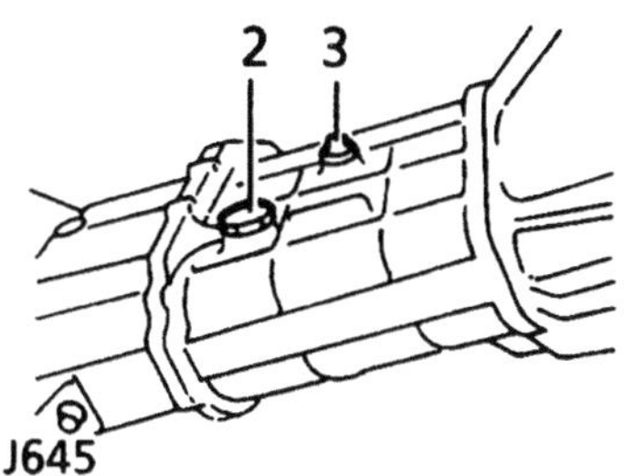

- Clean the area surrounding the drain plug (2) and filler level plug (3), to prevent contamination of the gearbox.

- Remove the drain plug (2) and allow the oil to drain completely.

- Clean and refit the drain plug.

- Remove the filler level plug (3) and inject the correct grade of oil (see 'General data') until it begins to run from the hole.

WARNING

Use only NEW oil - DO NOT use oil previously drained from the system.

- Clean and refit the filler level plug.

- Wipe any surplus oil from the area and remove the wheel chocks.

TRANSFER GEARBOX OIL RENEWAL

For safety, DO NOT work underneath the vehicle unless it is safely parked with the wheels chocked, or is supported by heavy duty stands.

Extreme care should be taken when draining gearbox oil, it may be hot and cause severe scalding.

Ensure the vehicle is parked on firm, level ground and chock the wheels. Place a suitable container under the gearbox to catch the used oil.

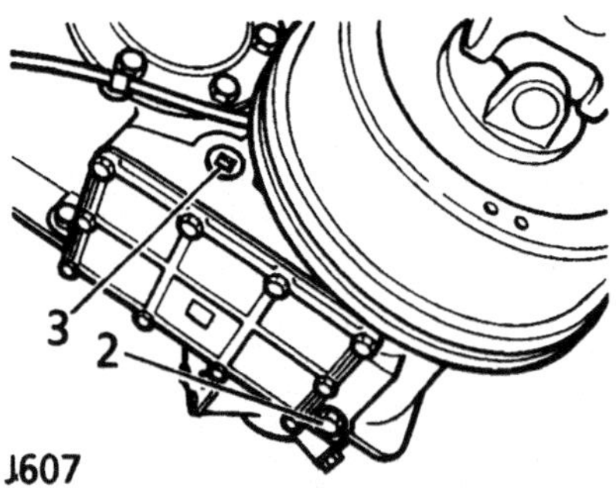

- Clean the area surrounding the drain plug (2) and filler level (3) plug, to prevent contamination of the gearbox.

- Remove the drain plug (2) and allow the oil to drain completely.

- Clean and refit the plug with a new washer. Tighten to a torque of 30 Nm (23 lbf/ft).

- Remove the filler level plug (3) and inject the correct grade of oil (see 'General data') until it begins to run from the hole.

Use only NEW oil - DO NOT use oil previously drained from the system.

- Clean and refit the filler level plug. Tighten to a torque of 30 Nm (23 lbf/ft).

- Wipe any surplus oil from the area and remove the wheel chocks.

FRONT/REAR AXLE OIL RENEWAL

WARNING

For safety, DO NOT work underneath the vehicle unless it is safely parked with the wheels chocked, or is supported by heavy duty stands.

Extreme care should be taken when draining axle oil, it may be hot and cause severe scalding.

NOTE: *A front axle is illustrated, but the procedure is the same for both axles.*

Ensure the vehicle is parked on firm, level ground and chock the wheels. Place a suitable container under the axle to be drained to catch the used oil.

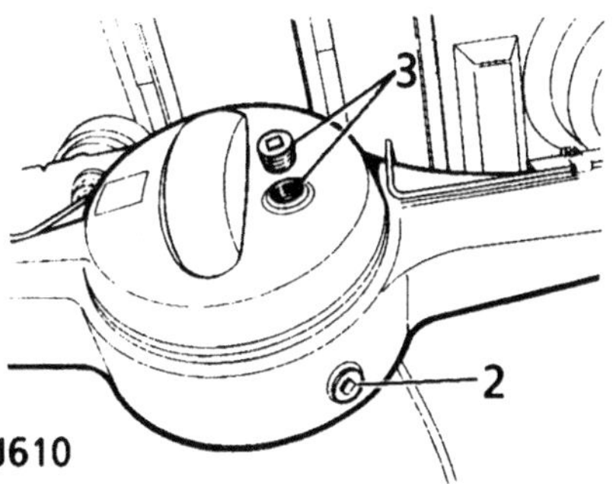

- Clean the area surrounding the drain plug (2) and filler level plug (3), to prevent contamination of the axles.

- Remove the drain plug (2) and allow the oil to drain completely.

- Clean and refit the drain plug.

- Remove the filler level plug (3) and inject the correct grade of oil (see 'General data') until it begins to run from the hole.

WARNING

Use only NEW oil - DO NOT use oil previously drained from the system.

- Clean and refit the filler level plug.

- Wipe any surplus oil from the area and remove the wheel chocks.

STEERING SWIVEL HOUSING OIL RENEWAL

WARNING

For safety, DO NOT work underneath the vehicle unless it is safely parked with the wheels chocked, or is supported by heavy duty stands.

Ensure the vehicle is parked on firm, level ground and chock the wheels. Place a suitable container under each swivel housing to catch the used oil.

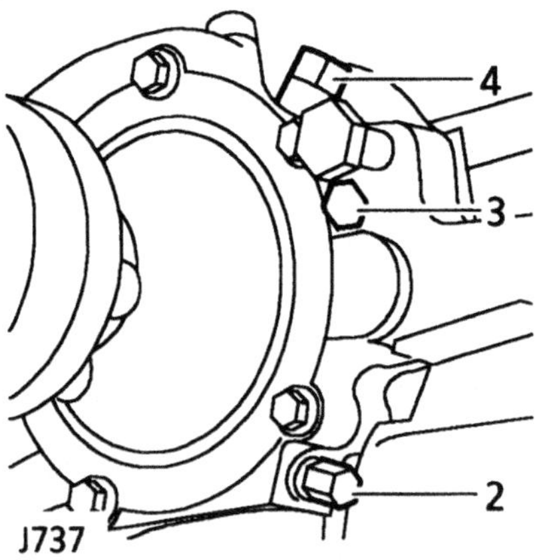

- Clean the area surrounding the drain plug (2), level plug (3) and filler plug (4), to prevent contamination.

- Remove the drain plug (2) and filler plug (4) to allow the oil to drain completely.

- Clean and refit the drain plug.

- Remove the level plug (3) and inject the correct grade of oil until it begins to run from the hole.

WARNING

Use only NEW oil - DO NOT use oil previously drained from the system.

- Clean and refit both the filler and level plugs.

- Wipe any surplus oil from the area and remove the wheel chocks.

- Repeat the procedure on the other swivel housing.

NOTE: *On later models, both the level plug and filler plug have been deleted. The assembly is injected with grease at manufacture and is maintenance free.*

BRAKE PAD, DISC AND CALIPER CHECK

If the vehicle is being operated in arduous conditions, especially when deep mud and/or wading situations are regularly encountered, the condition of the brake pads, discs and calipers should be checked at least weekly, if not even more frequently.

Hydraulic disc brakes are fitted to the front and rear wheels, they are self adjusting and therefore, no provision for manual adjustment is made.

- Check the thickness of the brake pads, which should not be less than 3mm (0.125 in).

- Check for uneven brake pad wear.

- Check for oil contamination on the brake discs and pads.

- Check condition of the brake discs for wear and/or corrosion.

- Check the brake calipers for any leaking brake fluid.

If necessary, any replacement or rectification of discs, brakes or calipers, should be carried out by a Land Rover dealer.

HANDBRAKE CHECK/ADJUSTMENT

For safety, DO NOT work underneath the vehicle unless it is safely parked with the wheels chocked, or is supported by heavy duty stands.

Ensure the vehicle is parked on firm, level ground and chock the wheels.

If the parking brake movement is excessive, adjust as follows:

- Raise one rear wheel clear of the ground and ensure it is supported securely with an axle stand.

- Release the handbrake.

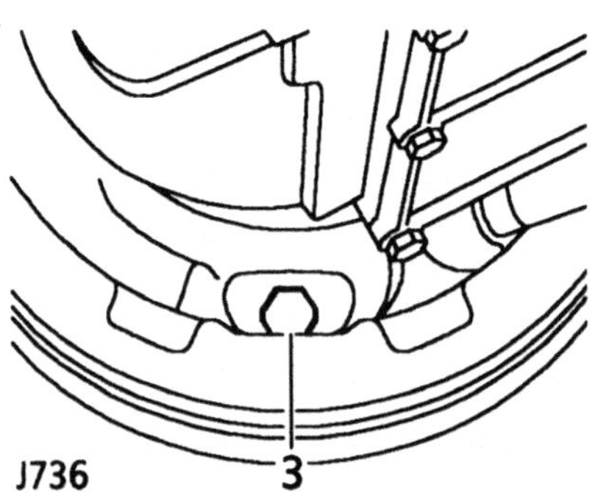

- Tighten the adjusting bolt (3) until brake drum will not rotate (by hand).

- Further tighten the adjusting bolt to a torque of 25 Nm (18 lbf/ft) to ensure that the brake drum is locked - if this is not the case, consult a Land Rover dealer.

- Finally, slacken the adjusting bolt by turning it 1.5 turns anti-clockwise.

The brake drum should now be free to rotate, and the brakes shoes correctly adjusted.

PROPELLER SHAFT LUBRICATION

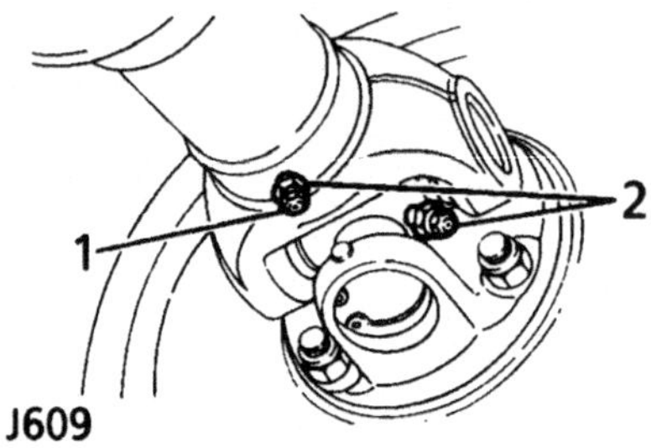

- Clean all the grease nipples on the front and rear propshaft universal joints (1). Charge a low pressure hand grease gun with the recommended grade of grease (see 'General data') and apply to the grease nipples (2).

Any additional greasing of the propshaft MUST be carried out by an authorised Land Rover dealer.

SECTION 6
General data

General data

LUBRICANTS AND FLUIDS

Recommendations for all climates and conditions.

COMPONENTS Specification	SAE	AMBIENT TEMPERATURE °C -30 -20 -10 0 10 20 30 40 50
Petrol engine sump		
Oils must meet	5W/30	
RES.22.0L.G4 or	5W/40, 5W/50	
ACEA A2:96	10W/30	
or API service levels SG or SH	10W/40,	
	10W/50	
	10W/60	
Diesel engine sump	5W/30	
	5W/40, 5W/50	
Diesel oils meeting		
RES 22.0L.PD2 or	10W/30	
ACEA B2:96 (or API CE)	10W/40	
	10W/50	
	15W/40	
Main gearbox		
ATF Dexron II D		
Transfer gearbox		
MIL-L-2105 or	90W EP	
MIL-L-2105B, C & D	80W EP	
Final drive units, swivel pin housings		
MIL-L-2105 or	90W EP	
MIL-L-2105B, C & D	80W EP	
Power steering		
ATF M2C 33 (F or G) or L		
ATF Dexron II D		

Lubrication nipples (hubs, ball joints, prop. shafts, etc.)
NLGI-2 Multipurpose Lithium based grease

Battery terminals
Petroleum jelly. DO NOT use silicone grease

Brake and clutch reservoirs
Universal brake fluids or any brake fluid having a minimum boiling point of 260° C
(500° F) and complying with FMVSS 116 DOT4

Windscreen washers
Screen washer fluid

Engine cooling system (petrol & diesel models)
Ethylene glycol based anti-freeze (containing no methanol) with non-phosphate corrosion
inhibitors suitable for use in aluminium engines. Use one part anti-freeze to one part water
for protection down to -33° F (-36° C)

Air conditioning compressor
Nippondenso ND-8 or Unipart ND-8

Door locks (anti-burst) and inertia reels
DO NOT LUBRICATE. These components are lubricated for life during manufacture.

CAPACITIES

The following capacities are approximate and provided as a guide only. All oil levels must be set using the dipstick or level plugs as applicable.

Fuel tank - usable capacity
- rear (110 & 130 models) .... 79,50 litre (17.50 gall)
- side (except 110 SW) .... 68,20 litre (15.00 gall)
- side (110 SW only) .... 45,50 litre (10.00 gall)
- side (90 models) .... 54,58 litre (12.00 gall)

Engine sump
- Tdi models .... 5,80 litre (10.15 pt)
- V8 petrol models .... 5,10 litre (9.00 pt)
- 4-cylinder models .... 6,00 litre (10.56 pt)

Additional capacity after fitting new oil filter
- Tdi models .... 0,85 litre (1.50 pt)
- V8 petrol models .... 0,56 litre (1.00 pt)
- 4-cylinder models .... 0,85 litre (1.50 pt)

Gearbox
- R380 .... 2,67 litre (4.70 pt)
Transfer box .... 2,30 litre (4.00 pt)
Front differential .... 1,70 litre (3.00 pt)
Rear differential
- (90 models) .... 1,70 litre (3.00 pt)
- (110 models) .... 2,26 litre (4.00 pt)

Cooling system,
- Tdi models .... 11,10 litre (20.00 pt)
- V8 petrol models .... 12,80 litre (22.50 pt)
- 4-cylinder models .... 10,80 litre (19.00 pt)

General data

Engine - Tdi

Bore .... 90,47 mm (3.562 in)
Stroke .... 97,00 mm (3.819 in)
Number of cylinders 4
Cylinder capacity .... 2495 cc (152 cu in)
Compression ratio 19.5:1
Firing order 1, 3, 4, 2
Injection timing .... 1,54 mm lift at T.D.C.
Tappet clearance, inlet .... 0,20 mm (0.008 in)
Tappet clearance, exhaust.................... 0,20 mm (0.008 in)   } Engine hot or cold
Valve timing (No. 1 exhaust valve peak) .... 109°

Engine - diesel (non-turbo)

Bore .... 90,47 mm (3.562 in)
Stroke .... 97,00 mm (3.819 in)
Number of cylinders 4
Cylinder capacity .... 2495 cc (152 cu in)
Compression ratio 21.0:1
Firing order 1, 3, 4, 2
Injection timing .... Set
Tappet clearance, inlet .... 0.25 mm (0.010 in)
Tappet clearance, exhaust.................... 0.25 mm (0.010 in)   } Engine hot or cold
Valve timing (No.1 exhaust valve peak) .... 106° to 109°

Engine - V8 petrol

Bore .... 88,90 mm (3.500 in)
Stroke .... 71,12 mm (2.800 in)
Number of cylinders 8
Cylinder capacity .... 3528 cc (215 cu in)
Compression ratio 9.35:1
Firing order 1, 8, 4, 3, 6, 5, 7, 2
Sparking plug type .... Champion RN9YC
Sparking plug gap .... 0,72 to 0,88 mm (0.028 to 0.035 in)
Distributor .... Electronic
Ignition timing, dynamic; .... 4° BTDC ± 1° with vacuum pipe disconnected

Engine - 4-cylinder petrol

Bore .... 90,47 mm (3.562 in)
Stroke .... 97,00 mm (3.819 in)
Number of cylinders 4
Cylinder capacity .... 2495 cc (152 cu in)
Compression ratio 8.0:1
Firing order 1,3,4,2
Sparking plug type .... Champion N9YC
Sparking plug gap .... 0,72 to 0,88 mm (0.028 to 0.035 in)
Distributor contact breaker gap .... 0,35 to 0,40 mm (0.014 to 0. 016 in)
Ignition timing, dynamic; .... 16° BDTC − 1° with vacuum pipe disconnected

STEERING (lock to lock)

Manual	4.3 turns
Power assisted	3.38 turns
Camber angle	Zero
Castor angle	3°
Swivel pin inclination	7°
Front wheel toe-out	0 to 2 mm

Turning circle between kerbs:

90 models:

- 750 x 16 tyres	11,7 m (38.4 ft)
- 205 x 16 tyres	11,7 m (38.4 ft)
- 265/75 x 16 tyres	12,65 m (41.5 ft)

110 models:

- 750 x 16 tyres	13,41 m (44 ft)

130 models:

- 750 x 16 tyres	15,24 m (50 ft)

ELECTRICAL SYSTEM

Type	Negative earth
Voltage	12

Battery

- Tdi models	380/120/90
- non-turbo diesel models	490/170/90
- petrol models	210/85/90
Charging circuit	Alternator

Ignition system

- petrol models	Coil

REPLACEMENT BULBS

Headlights	60/55 W Halogen bulb
Front side lights	12 V 5 W
Side repeater lights	12 V 5 W
Stop lights	12 V 21 W
Tail lights	12 V 5 W
Direction indicator lights	12 V 21 W
Number plate lights	12 V 4 W
Reversing lights	12 V 21 W
Rear fog guard lights	12 V 21 W
Interior lights	12 V 10 W

General data

DIMENSIONS

90 models

Overall length:
- Soft top & Pick-up .... 3722 mm (146.5 in)
- Hard top & Station wagon .... 3883 mm (152.9 in)

Overall width .... 1790 mm (70.5 in)

Overall height:
- Soft top .... 1965 mm (77.4 in)
- Pick-up & Station wagon .... 1963 mm (77.3 in)
- Hard top .... 1972 mm (77.6 in)

Wheelbase .... 2360 mm (92.9 in)
Track front/rear .... 1486 mm (58.5 in)
Width between wheel boxes .... 925 mm (36.4 in)

110 models

Overall length:
- Soft top & Pick-up .... 4438 mm (175 in)
- High capacity pick-up .... 4631 mm (182 in)
- Hard top/Station wagon & County .... 4599 mm (181 in)

Overall width .... 1790 mm (70.5 in)
Overall height .... 2035 mm (80.1 in)
Wheelbase .... 2794 mm (110 in)
Track front/rear .... 1486 mm (58.5 in)

Width between wheel boxes:
- High capacity pick-up .... 1090 mm (43 in)
- all other models .... 925 mm (36.4 in)

General data

130 models

Overall length	5132 mm (202 in)
Overall width	1790 mm (70.5 in)
Overall height	2035 mm (80.1 in)
Wheelbase	3226 mm (127 in)
Track front/rear	1486 mm (58.5 in)
Width between wheel boxes	1090 mm (43 in)

OFF-ROAD PERFORMANCE

90 models

Max. gradient (EEC kerb weight) .... 45°

Approach angle:
- Soft top & Pick-up (EEC kerb weight) .... 48°
- Hard top & Station wagon (EEC kerb weight) ...... 51.5°

Departure angle
- Soft top & Pick-up (EEC kerb weight) .... 49°
- Hard top & Station wagon (EEC kerb weight) ...... 53°

Wading depth .... 500 mm (20 in)

Min. ground clearance (unladen):
- Soft top & Pick-up .... 191 mm (7.5 in)
- Hard top & Station wagon .... 229 mm (9.0 in)

NOTE: *Departure angles do not account for the addition of a tow hitch.*

110 & 130 models

Max. gradient (EEC kerb weight) .... 45°
Approach angle (EEC kerb weight) .... 50°

Departure angle (EEC kerb weight)
110 models .... 35°
130 models .... 34°

Wading depth .... 500 mm (20 in)
Min. ground clearance (unladen) .... 215 mm (8.5 in)

NOTE: *Departure angles do not account for the addition of a tow hitch.*

TOWING WEIGHTS

4-cyl petrol, V8 & 300Tdi models	**On-road**	**Off-road**
- Unbraked trailers	750 kg (1653 lb)	500 kg (1102 lb)
- Trailers with overrun brakes	3500 kg (7716 lb)	1000 kg (2204 lb)
- 4 wheel trailers with coupled brakes*	4000 kg (8818 lb)	1000 kg (2204 lb)

4-cyl diesel non-turbo models		
- Unbraked trailers	750 kg (1653 lb)	500 kg (1102 lb)
- Trailers with overrun brakes	3500 kg (7716 lb)	1000 kg (2204 lb)
- 4 wheel trailers with coupled brakes*	3500 kg (7716 lb)	1000 kg (2204 lb)

Nose weight	75 kg (165 lb)	75 kg (165 lb)

NOTE: * Only applies to vehicles modified to accept coupled brakes.

NOTE: All weight figures are subject to local restrictions.

VEHICLE WEIGHTS

90 models	Standard	High load
Max front axle weight	1200 kg (2645 lb)	1200 kg (2645 lb)
Max rear axle weight	1380 kg (3042 lb)	1500 kg (3307 lb)
Gross vehicle weight	2400 kg (5291 lb)	2550 kg (5622 lb)

110 models	Levelled	Unlevelled
Max front axle weight	1200 kg (2645 lb)	1200 kg (2645 lb)
Max rear axle weight	1750 kg (3858 lb)	1850 kg (4078 lb)
Gross vehicle weight	2950 kg (6503 lb)	3050 kg (6724 lb)

130 models	
Max front axle weight	1580 kg (3483 lb)
Max rear axle weight	2200 kg (4850 lb)
Gross vehicle weight	3500 kg (7716 lb)

NOTE: Axle weights are non additive. The individual maximum axle weights and gross vehicle weight must not be exceeded.

General data

EEC KERB WEIGHT

90 models	Standard	High load
Soft top:		
- 4-cyl petrol	1636 kg (3606 lb)	1640 kg (3615 lb)
- V8 petrol	1627 kg (3587 lb)	1627 kg (3587 lb)
- 4-cyl diesel	1656 kg (3650 lb)	1660 kg (3659 lb)
- Tdi	1695 kg (3736 lb)	1699 kg (3745 lb)
Pick-up:		
- 4-cyl petrol	1636 kg (3606 lb)	1640 kg (3615 lb)
- V8 petrol	1627 kg (3587 lb)	1627 kg (3587 lb)
- 4-cyl diesel	1665 kg (3670 lb)	1669 kg (3679 lb)
- Tdi	1694 kg (3734 lb)	1698 kg (3743 lb)
Hard top:		
- 4-cyl petrol	1683 kg (3710 lb)	1687 kg (3719 lb)
- V8 petrol	1672 kg (3686 lb)	1672 kg (3686 lb)
- 4-cyl diesel	1703 kg (3754 lb)	1707 kg (3763 lb)
- Tdi	1746 kg (3849 lb)	1750 kg (3858 lb)
Station wagon:		
- 4-cyl petrol	1701 kg (3750 lb)	1705 kg (3758 lb)
- V8 petrol	1690 kg (3725 lb)	1690 kg (3725 lb)
- 4-cyl diesel	1721 kg (3794 lb)	1725 kg (3803 lb)
- Tdi	1793 kg (3952 lb)	1797 kg (3961 lb)

EEC kerb weight = Unladen weight + Full fuel tank + 75 kg driver.

EEC KERB WEIGHT

110 models	Levelled	Unlevelled
Soft top:		
- 4-cyl petrol	1805 kg (3979 lb)	1815 kg (4001 lb)
- V8 petrol	1806 kg (3981 lb)	1816 kg (4003 lb)
- 4-cyl diesel	1828 kg (4030 lb)	1838 kg (4052 lb)
- Tdi	1872 kg (4127 lb)	1882 kg (4149 lb)
Pick-up:		
- 4-cyl petrol	1815 kg (4001 lb)	1825 kg (4023 lb)
- V8 petrol	1815 kg (4001 lb)	1825 kg (4023 lb)
- 4-cyl diesel	1839 kg (4054 lb)	1849 kg (4076 lb)
- Tdi	1880 kg (4144 lb)	1890 kg (4166 lb)
H.C. pick-up:		
- 4-cyl petrol	1853 kg (4085 lb)	1863 kg (4107 lb)
- V8 petrol	1853 kg (4085 lb)	1863 kg (4107 lb)
- 4-cyl diesel	1877 kg (4138 lb)	1887 kg (4160 lb)
- Tdi	1917 kg (4226 lb)	1927 kg (4248 lb)
Hard top:		
- 4-cyl petrol	1840 kg (4056 lb)	1850 kg (4078 lb)
- V8 petrol	1840 kg (4056 lb)	1850 kg (4078 lb)
- 4-cyl diesel	1867 kg (4116 lb)	1877 kg (4138 lb)
- Tdi	1913 kg (4217 lb)	1923 kg (4239 lb)
Station wagon:		
- 4-cyl petrol	1943 kg (4283 lb)	1953 kg (4305 lb)
- V8 petrol	1944 kg (4285 lb)	1954 kg (4307 lb)
- 4-cyl diesel	1969 kg (4340 lb)	1979 kg (4362 lb)
- Tdi	2018 kg (4448 lb)	2028 kg (4470 lb)
County S.W:		
- 4-cyl petrol	1979 kg (4362 lb)	1989 kg (4385 lb)
- V8 petrol	1980 kg (4365 lb)	1990 kg (4387 lb)
- 4-cyl diesel	2005 kg (4420 lb)	2015 kg (4442 lb)
- Tdi	2054 kg (4528 lb)	2064 kg (4550 lb)

EEC kerb weight = Unladen weight + Full fuel tank + 75 kg driver.

EEC KERB WEIGHT

130 models

Crew cab & H.C. pick-up
- V8 petrol .... 2012 kg (4435 lb)
- Tdi .... 2086 kg (4598 lb)

EEC kerb weight = Unladen weight + Full fuel tank + 75 kg driver.

FUEL CONSUMPTION

The fuel consumption figures shown below have been calculated using a standard testing procedure (the new EC test procedure from Directive 93/116/EC), and produced in accordance with The Passenger Car Fuel Consumption (Amendment) Order 1996. Under normal use, a car's actual fuel consumption figures may differ from those achieved through the test procedure, depending on driving technique, road and traffic conditions, environmental factors, vehicle and load conditions.

	URBAN		EXTRA-URBAN		COMBINED	
	mpg	l/100km	mpg	l/100km	mpg	l/100km
90 models:						
300 TDi	24.2	11.8	32.5	8.7	28.8	9.8
110 & 130 models:						
300 TDi	22.7	12.5	32.4	8.7	27.9	10.1

Urban cycle

The urban test cycle is carried out from a cold start and consists of a series of accelerations, decelerations and periods of steady speed driving and engine idling. The maximum speed attained during the test is 31 mph (50 km/h), with an average speed of 12 mph (19 km/h).

Extra-urban cycle

The extra-urban test cycle is carried out immediately after the urban test. Approximately half the test comprises steady speed driving, while the remainder consists of a series of accelerations, decelerations and engine idling. The maximum test speed is 75 mph (120 km/h) and the average speed 39 mph (63 km/h). The test is carried out over a distance of 4.3 miles (7 km).

Combined

The combined figure is an average of the urban and the extra-urban test cycle results, which has been weighted to take account of the different distances covered during the two tests.

NOTE: *These figures should not be compared with the figures produced using the ECE/EEC procedure previously required by The Passenger Car Fuel Consumption Order 1983. Because of the changes in test procedure, even the urban figures would differ if the same car were subjected to both tests.*

TYRE SIZE AND PRESSURES

90 models:	**Front**	**Rear**
Normal - all load conditions		
205 R16 radial	1,9 bar	2,4 bar
& 265/75 R16 radial (multi-terrain)	28 lbf/in^2	35 lbf/in^2
	2,0 kgf/cm^2	2,5 kgf/cm^2
750 R16 radial	1,9 bar	2,75 bar
	28 lbf/in^2	40 lbf/in^2
	2,0 kgf/cm^2	2,8 kgf/cm^2

<table>
<tr><td>

WARNING

Tyre pressures must be checked with the tyres cold, as the pressure is about 0.21 bar (3 lbf/in^2) 0.2 kgf/cm^2 higher at running temperature. If the vehicle has been parked in the sun or high ambient temperatures, DO NOT reduce the tyre pressures, move the vehicle into the shade and wait for the tyres to cool before checking the pressures.

</td><td>

WARNING

ALWAYS use the same make and type of radial-ply tyres, front and rear. DO NOT use cross-ply tyres, or interchange tyres from front to rear.

- *If the wheel is marked 'TUBED', an inner tube MUST be fitted, even with a tubeless tyre.*

- *If the wheel is marked 'TUBELESS', an inner tube must NOT be fitted.*

</td></tr>
</table>

110 models:	Front	Rear
750 R16 Radial		
Normal - all load conditions	1,9 bar	3,3 bar
	28 lbf/in²	48 lbf/in²
	2,0 kgf/cm²	3,4 kgf/cm²

130 models:		
750 R16 Radial		
Normal - all load conditions	3,0 bar	4,5 bar
	44 lbf/in²	65 lbf/in²
	3,1 kgf/cm²	4,6 kgf/cm²

WARNING

Tyre pressures must be checked with the tyres cold, as the pressure is about 0.21 bar (3 lbf/in², 0.2 kgf/cm²) higher at running temperature. If the vehicle has been parked in the sun or high ambient temperatures, DO NOT reduce the tyre pressures, move the vehicle into the shade and wait for the tyres to cool before checking the pressures.

WARNING

ALWAYS use the same make and type of radial-ply tyres, front and rear. DO NOT use cross-ply tyres, or interchange tyres from front to rear.

- *If the wheel is marked 'TUBED', an inner tube MUST be fitted, even with a tubeless tyre.*

- *If the wheel is marked 'TUBELESS', an inner tube must NOT be fitted.*

SECTION 7
Parts & accessories

PARTS AND ACCESSORIES

Your vehicle has been designed, manufactured and proven to cope with the most rigorous driving conditions. As such, fitting parts and accessories that have been developed and tested to the same stringent standards is essential to guarantee the continued reliability, safety and performance of the vehicle.

To augment the vehicles' already awesome ability, a comprehensive and versatile range of quality spare parts and accessories are available to fulfil a wide variety of roles, both enhancing and protecting the vehicle in the many tasks to which it can be applied.

Genuine Land Rover Parts are the ONLY parts built to original equipment specifications AND approved by Land Rover designers - this means that every single part and accessory has been rigorously tested by the same engineering team that designed and built the vehicle and can therefore be GUARANTEED for twelve months with UNLIMITED MILEAGE.

A full list and description of all available accessories is available from your Land Rover dealer.

Always consult your dealer for advice regarding the approval, suitability, installation and use of any parts or accessories before fitting.

WARNING

The fitting of parts and accessories of inferior quality, or the carrying out of non-approved conversions, may be dangerous and could affect the safety of the vehicle and occupants and invalidate the terms and conditions of the vehicle warranty.

Always consult a Land Rover dealer before fitting accessories, and before commencing any conversion or alteration to the vehicles' original specification.

Electrical equipment

WARNING

It is extremely hazardous to fit or replace parts or accessories whose installation requires the dismantling of or addition to either the electrical or fuel system.

Fitting inferior quality parts or accessories, may be dangerous and could invalidate the vehicle warranty.

After sales service

The After Sales Parts service is of paramount importance, both in the UK and across the world. In the UK there are over 100 authorised Land Rover dealers, all computer linked for rapid ordering of parts and accessories.

In addition, with franchised representation in over 100 countries worldwide, Land Rover are able to support your vehicle wherever you go.

A full list of Land Rover dealers is included in the literature pack.

Only Land Rover dealers are able to provide the full range of recommended parts and accessories that meet our rigorous standards of safety, durability and performance.

Travelling abroad

In certain countries, it is illegal to fit parts which have not been made to the vehicle manufacturers' specification.

Owners should ensure that any parts or accessories fitted to the vehicle while travelling abroad, will conform to the legal requirements of their own country when they return home.

This section of the handbook is devoted to your vehicle's superb off-road driving capabilities.

Before venturing off-road however, it is *absolutely essential* that inexperienced drivers become fully familiar with the vehicle's controls, in particular the transfer gearbox, and also study the off-road driving techniques described on the following pages.

Off-road driving

BASIC OFF-ROAD TECHNIQUES

These basic driving techniques are an introduction to the art of off-road driving and do not necessarily provide the information needed to successfully cope with every single off-road situation.

We strongly recommend that owners who intend to drive off-road frequently, should seek as much additional information and practical experience as possible.

Gear selection

Correct gear selection is possibly the single most important factor for safe and successful off-road driving. While only experience will tell you which is the correct gear for any section of ground, the following basic rules apply:

1. NEVER change gear or de-clutch while negotiating difficult terrain - the drag on the wheels may cause the vehicle to stop when the clutch is depressed and restarting may be difficult.

2. Generally, and especially where slippery or soft ground conditions prevail, the higher the gear you select the better.

3. When descending very steep slopes always select 1st gear in LOW range.

Inexperienced drivers are advised to stop the vehicle and carefully consider which gear will be most appropriate for each manoeuvre before continuing.

Slipping the clutch

Use of excessive clutch slip to prevent the engine stalling will result in premature clutch wear. Always select a gear low enough to enable the vehicle to proceed without the need to slip the clutch.

DO NOT drive with your foot resting on the clutch pedal; driving across uneven terrain could cause you to inadvertently depress the clutch, resulting in loss of control of the vehicle.

Transfer gears

High range gears should be used whenever possible - only change to low range when ground conditions become very difficult. The DIFF LOCK should be engaged whenever there is a risk of losing wheel grip, and disengaged as soon as firm, level, non-slippery ground is reached.

Braking

As far as possible, vehicle speed should be controlled through correct gear selection. Application of the brake pedal should be kept to an absolute minimum. Harsh braking on wet, muddy or loose surfaces could prove dangerous.

NOTE: If the correct gear has been selected, braking will be largely unnecessary.

Use of engine for braking

Before descending steep slopes, stop the vehicle at least a length before the descent, select neutral in the main gearbox, engage LOW range and then select first or second gear depending on the severity of the incline.

While descending the slope it should be remembered that the engine will provide sufficient braking effort to control the rate of descent, and that the brakes should not be applied.

Accelerating

Use the accelerator with care - any sudden surge of power may induce wheel spin and result in loss of control of the vehicle.

Steering

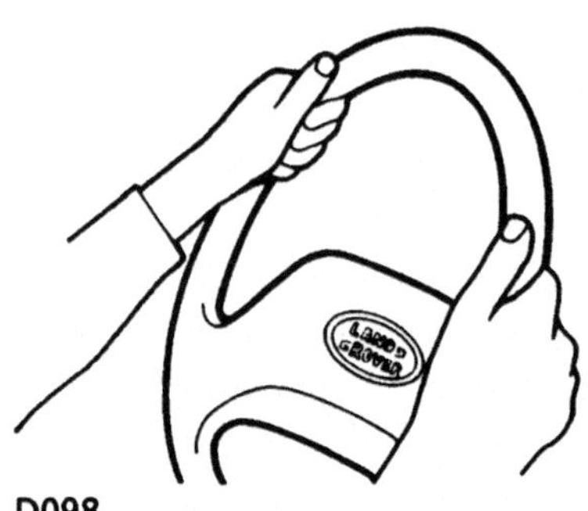

D098

WARNING

DO NOT hold the steering wheel with your thumbs inside the rim - a sudden 'kick' of the wheel as the vehicle negotiates a rut or boulder could seriously injure them. ALWAYS grip the wheel on the outside of the rim (as shown) when traversing uneven ground.

Survey the ground before driving

Before negotiating difficult terrain, it is wise to carry out a preliminary survey on foot. This will minimise the risk of your vehicle getting into difficulty through a previously unnoticed hazard.

Off-road driving

Ground clearance

Don't forget to allow for ground clearance beneath the chassis, and under the front and rear bumpers. Note that the axle differentials are situated BELOW the chassis and are positioned slightly to the RIGHT of the centre of the vehicle. Note also that there are other parts of the vehicle which may come into contact with the ground; take care not to ground the vehicle.

Ground clearance is particularly important at the bottom of steep a slope, or where wheel ruts are unusually deep and where sudden changes in the slope of the ground are experienced.

On soft ground the axle differentials will clear their own path in all but the most difficult conditions. However, on frozen, rocky or hard ground, hard contact between the differentials and the ground will generally result in the vehicle coming to a sudden stop.

Always attempt to avoid obstacles that may foul the chassis or axle differentials.

Loss of traction

If the vehicle is immobile due to loss of wheel grip, the following hints could be of value:

- Avoid prolonged wheel spin; this will make matters worse.

- Remove obstacles rather than forcing the vehicle across them.

- Clear clogged tyre treads.

- Reverse as far as possible, then attempt an increased speed approach - additional momentum may overcome the obstacle.

- Brushwood, sacking or any similar material placed in front of the tyres will improve tyre grip.

IMPORTANT INFORMATION

After driving off-road

Before rejoining the public highway, or driving at speeds above 40 km/h (25 mph), consideration should be given to the following:

- Wheels and tyres must be cleaned of mud and inspected for damage - ensure there are no lumps or bulges in the tyres or exposure of the ply or cord structure.

- Brake discs and calipers should be examined and any stones or grit that may affect braking efficiency removed.

Servicing requirements

Vehicles operating in arduous conditions, particularly on dusty, muddy, or wet terrain, and vehicles undergoing frequent or deep wading conditions will require more frequent servicing. See 'Owner maintenance' and contact a Land Rover dealer for advice.

In addition:

After wading in salt water or driving on sandy beaches, use a hose to thoroughly wash the underbody components and any exposed body panels with fresh water. This will help to protect the vehicle's cosmetic appearance.

Off-road driving

DRIVING ON SOFT SURFACES & DRY SAND

The ideal technique for driving on soft ground and dry sand, requires the vehicle to be kept moving at all times - soft ground and sand causes excessive drag on the wheels, resulting in a rapid loss of motion once driving momentum is lost. For this reason, gear changing should be avoided.

- Engage the DIFF LOCK.

- Select the highest suitable gear and REMAIN in that gear until a firm surface is reached. It is generally advisable to use LOW range gears, as these will enable you to accelerate through worsening conditions without the risk of being unable to restart.

- Disengage the DIFF LOCK as soon as firm ground is reached.

Stopping the vehicle on soft ground, in sand or on an incline

If you do stop your vehicle, remember:

Starting on an incline or in soft ground or sand is almost impossible. Always park on a firm level area, or with the vehicle facing downhill.

To avoid wheel spin, select second or third gear, and use the MINIMUM throttle necessary to get the vehicle moving.

If forward motion is lost, avoid excessive use of the throttle - this will cause wheel spin and tend to dig the vehicle into the sand. Clear sand from around the tyres and ensure that the chassis and axles are not bearing on the sand before again attempting to move.

If the wheels have sunk, use an air bag lifting device or high lift jack to raise the vehicle, and then build up sand under the wheels so that the vehicle is again on level ground. If a restart is still not possible, place sand mats or ladders beneath the wheels.

Off-road driving

DRIVING ON SLIPPERY SURFACES
(ice, snow, mud, wet grass)

- With the DIFF LOCK engaged, select the highest gear possible.

- Drive away using the MINIMUM possible throttle opening.

- Drive slowly at all times, keeping braking to a minimum and avoiding violent movements of the steering wheel.

- Disengage the DIFF LOCK as soon as a non slippery surface is reached.

DRIVING ON ROUGH TRACKS

Although rough tracks can sometimes be negotiated in normal drive, it is advisable to lock the differential if excessive suspension movement is likely to induce wheel spin.

On very rough tracks, engage LOW range to enable a steady, low speed to be maintained without constant use of the brake and clutch pedals.

Always disengage the DIFF LOCK when smooth, firm ground is reached.

Off-road driving

CLIMBING STEEP SLOPES

Engage the DIFF LOCK and ALWAYS follow the fall line of the slope - travelling diagonally could encourage the vehicle to slide broadside down the slope.

Steep climbs will usually require the LOW gear range. If the surface is loose or slippery, use sufficient speed in the highest practical gear to take advantage of the vehicle's momentum. However, too high a speed over a bumpy surface may result in a wheel lifting, causing the vehicle to lose traction. In this case try a slower approach. Traction can also be improved by easing off the accelerator just before loss of forward motion.

If the vehicle is unable to complete a climb, do not attempt to turn it around while on the slope. Instead, adopt the following procedure to reverse downhill to the foot of the slope:

1. Hold the vehicle stationary using both foot and hand brakes.

2. Restart the engine if necessary.

3. Engage reverse gear LOW range.

4. Release the handbrake. Then release the foot brake and clutch simultaneously, and allow the vehicle to reverse down the slope using engine braking to control the rate of descent.

5. Unless it is necessary to stop the vehicle in order to negotiate obstructions, DO NOT apply the brake or clutch pedal during the descent.

6. If the vehicle begins to slide, accelerate slightly to allow the tyres to regain grip.

When the vehicle is back on level ground or where traction can be regained, a faster approach will probably enable the hill to be climbed. However, DO NOT take unnecessary risks, if the hill is too difficult to climb, find an alternative route.

WARNING

The engine must be restarted before reversing down the slope, as there will be no servo assistance to the brakes unless the engine is running.

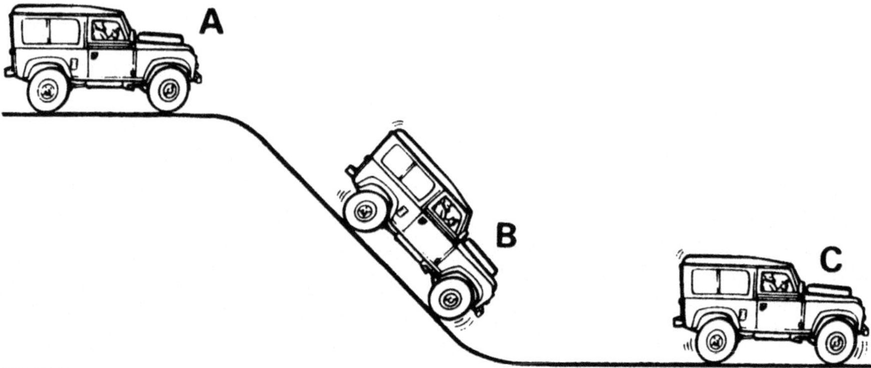

DESCENDING STEEP SLOPES

A. Stop the vehicle at least a vehicle length before the slope and engage first gear LOW range with the differential locked.

B. Unless it is necessary to stop the vehicle in order to negotiate obstructions, **DO NOT** touch the brake or clutch pedals during the descent - the engine will limit the speed, keeping the vehicle under control provided the front wheels are turning. If the vehicle begins to slide, accelerate gently to maintain directional stability - DO NOT use the brakes or attempt to change gear.

C. Once level ground is reached, unlock the differential and select a suitable gear for the next stage of your journey.

WARNING

Failure to follow these instructions may cause the vehicle to roll over.

TRAVERSING A SLOPE

Before crossing a slope, ALWAYS observe the following precautions:

- Check that the ground is firm and not slippery.

- Check that the wheels on the downhill side of the vehicle are not likely to drop into any depressions in the ground and that the 'uphill' wheels will not run over rocks, tree roots, or similar obstacles that could suddenly increase the angle of tilt.

- Ensure that passenger weight is evenly distributed, that all roof rack luggage is removed and that all other luggage is properly secured and stowed as low as possible. Always remember; any sudden movement of the load could cause the vehicle to overturn.

- Rear seat passengers should sit on the uphill side of the vehicle or, in extreme conditions, should vacate the vehicle until the sloping ground has been safely negotiated.

NEGOTIATING A 'V' SHAPED GULLY

Observe extreme caution! Steering up either of the gully walls could cause the side of the vehicle to be trapped against the opposite gully wall.

DRIVING IN EXISTING WHEEL TRACKS

As far as possible allow the vehicle to steer itself along the bottom of the ruts. However, always keep a light hold of the steering wheel to prevent it from spinning free.

Particularly in wet conditions, if the steering wheel is allowed to spin free, the vehicle may appear to be driving straight ahead in the ruts, but in actual fact (due to the lack of traction caused by the wet ground) is unknowingly on full right or left lock. Then, when level ground is reached, or if a dry patch is encountered, the wheels will find traction and cause the vehicle to suddenly veer to left or right.

CROSSING A RIDGE

Approach at right angles so that both front wheels and then both rear wheels cross the ridge together - an angled approach could cause traction to be lost through diagonally opposite wheels lifting from the ground at the same time.

CROSSING A DITCH

With the DIFF LOCK engaged, cross ditches at an angle so that three wheels always maintain contact with the ground (if approached head on, both front wheels will drop into the ditch together, possibly resulting in the chassis and front bumper being trapped on opposite sides of the ditch).

Off-road driving

WADING

WARNING

The maximum advisable wading depth is 0,5 metre (20 in.).
Severe electrical damage may occur if the vehicle remains stationary for any length of time when the water level is above the door sills.

If the water is likely to exceed 0,5 metre (20 in.) while the vehicle is moving, the following precautions MUST be observed:

- Fix a plastic sheet in front of the radiator grille to prevent water from soaking the engine and mud from blocking the radiator.

- Fit a drain plug to the flywheel housing and diesel engine timing cover - Tdi engines only (see 'Owner maintenance').

- Ensure that the silt bed beneath the water is firm enough to support the vehicle's weight and provide sufficient traction.

- Ensure that the engine air intake is clear of the water.

- To prevent saturation of the electrical system and air intake, avoid excessive engine speed.

- With the DIFF LOCK engaged, select a low gear and maintain sufficient throttle to prevent the engine from stalling. This is particularly important if the exhaust pipe is under water.

- Drive slowly into the water and accelerate to a speed which causes a bow wave to form; then maintain that speed.

At all times, keep all the doors fully closed.

After wading

- Drive the vehicle a short distance and apply the footbrake to check that the brakes are fully effective.

- DO NOT rely on the handbrake to hold the vehicle stationary until the transmission has thoroughly dried out; in the meantime, leave the vehicle parked in gear.

- Remove the timing cover drain plug (where fitted) and also any covering material from the front of the radiator grille.

- If the water was particularly muddy, remove any blockages (mud and leaves) from the radiator to reduce the risk of overheating.

- If deep water is regularly negotiated, check transmission oils for signs of water contamination - contaminated oil can be identified through its 'milky' appearance. In addition, check the air filter element for water ingress, and replace if wet.

- Vehicles required to undergo frequent or deep wading conditions will require more frequent servicing. See 'Owner maintenance' and contact a Land Rover dealer for advice.

- If salt water is frequently negotiated, thoroughly wash the underbody components and exposed body panels, with fresh water.

Index

Index

Index

Index

DEFENDER 90·110·130

Forecourt data

Fuel

Diesel engines:
Use ONLY diesel fuel (Automotive Gas Oil) not exceeding 1% sulphur content.

Petrol engines:
- 4-cylinder engines;
Use 90 RON minimum leaded or unleaded fuel.
- V8 engines:
Use 91-93 RON leaded or unleaded fuel.

NOTE: On petrol engines fitted with a catalytic converter, use UNLEADED 95 RON minimum fuel ONLY.

Fuel tank capacity

Side tank:

90 models	54,6 litres (12 gallons)
110 models (except SW)	68,2 litres (15 gallons)
110 Station wagon	45,5 litres (10 gallons)

Rear tank:

110 & 130 models	79,5 litres (17.5 gallons)

Engine oil

Diesel engines:
15W/40 oil (RES.22.OL.PD2 or ACEA B2:96 or API CE)

Petrol engines:
10W/40* (RES.22.OL.G4 or ACEA A2:96 or API SG or API SH)

* See 'General data' for full details

Front Tyre Pressures

	bar	lbf/in^2	kgf/cm^2
All load conditions			
90 models:			
205/265/750 R16	1,9	28	2,0
110 models:			
750 R16	1,9	28	2,0
130 models:			
750 R16	3,0	44	3,1

Rear Tyre Pressures

	bar	lbf/in^2	kgf/cm^2
All load conditions			
90 models:			
205/265 R16	2,4	35	2,5
750 R16	2,75	40	2,8
110 models:			
750 R16	3,3	48	3,4
130 models:			
750 R16	4,5	65	4,6

LAND ROVER OFFICIAL FACTORY PUBLICATIONS

Land Rover Series 1 Workshop Manual	4291
Land Rover Series 1 1948-53 Parts Catalogue	4051
Land Rover Series 1 1954-58 Parts Catalogue	4107
Land Rover Series 1 Instruction Manual	4277
Land Rover Series 1 and II Diesel Instruction Manual	4343
Land Rover Series II and IIA Workshop Manual	AKM8159
Land Rover Series II and Early IIA Bonneted Control Parts Catalogue	605957
Land Rover Series IIA Bonneted Control Parts Catalogue	RTC9840CC
Land Rover Series IIA, III and 109 V8 Optional Equipment Parts Catalogue	RTC9842CE
Land Rover Series IIA/IIB Instruction Manual	LSM64IM
Land Rover Series 2A and 3 88 Parts Catalogue Supplement (USA Spec)	606494
Land Rover Series III Workshop Manual	AKM3648
Land Rover Series III Workshop Manual V8 Supplement (edn. 2)	AKM8022
Land Rover Series III 88, 109 and 109 V8 Parts Catalogue	RTC9841CE
Land Rover Series III Owners Manual 1971-1978	607324B
Land Rover Series III Owners Manual 1979-1985	AKM8155
Military Land Rover (Lightweight) Series III Parts Catalogue	61278
Military Land Rover Series III (L.W.B.) User Handbook	608179
Military Land Rover (Lightweight) Series III User Manual	608180
Land Rover 90/110 and Defender Workshop Manual 1983-1992	SLR621ENWM
Land Rover Defender Workshop Manual 1993-1995	LDAWMEN93
Land Rover Defender 300 Tdi and Supplements Workshop Manual 1996-1998	LRL0097ENGBB
Land Rover Defender Td5 Workshop Manual and Supplements 1999-2006	LRL0410BB
Land Rover Defender Electrical Manual Td5 1999-06 and 300Tdi 2002-2006	LRD5EHBB
Land Rover 110 Parts Catalogue 1983-1986	RTC9863CE
Land Rover Defender Parts Catalogue 1987-2006	STC9021CC
Land Rover 90 • 110 Handbook 1983-1990 MY	LSM0054
Land Rover Defender 90 • 110 • 130 Handbook 1991 MY - Feb. 1994	LHAHBEN93
Land Rover Defender 90 • 110 • 130 Handbook Mar. 1994 - 1998 MY	LRL0087ENG/2
Military Land Rover 90/110 All Variants (Excluding APV and SAS) User Manual	2320-D-122-201
Military Land Rover 90 and 110 2.5 Diesel Engine Versions User Handbook	SLR989WDHB
Military Land Rover Defender XD - Wolf Workshop Manual - 2320D128 -	302 522 523 524
Military Land Rover Defender XD - Wolf Parts Catalogue	2320D128711
Discovery Workshop Manual 1990-1994 (petrol 3.5, 3.9, Mpi and diesel 200 Tdi)	SJR900ENWM
Discovery Workshop Manual 1995-1998 (petrol 2.0 Mpi, 3.9, 4.0 V8 and diesel 300 Tdi)	LRL0079BB
Discovery Series II Workshop Manual 1999-2003 (petrol 4.0 V8 and diesel Td5 2.5)	VDR100090/6
Discovery Parts Catalogue 1989-1998 (2.0 Mpi, 3.5, 3.9 V8 and 200 Tdi and 300 Tdi)	RTC9947CF
Discovery Parts Catalogue 1999-2003 (petrol 4.0 V8 and diesel Td5 2.5)	STC9049CA
Discovery Owners Handbook 1990-1991 (petrol 3.5 V8 and diesel 200 Tdi)	SJR820ENHB90
Discovery Series II Handbook 1999-2004 MY (petrol 4.0 V8 and Td5 diesel)	LRL0459BB
Freelander Workshop Manual 1998-2000 (petrol 1.8 and diesel 2.0)	LRL0144
Freelander Workshop Manual 2001-2003 ON (petrol 1.8L, 2.5L and diesel Td4 2.0)	LRL0350ENG/4
Land Rover 101 1 Tonne Forward Control Workshop Manual	RTC9120
Land Rover 101 1 Tonne Forward Control Parts Catalogue	608294B
Land Rover 101 1 Tonne Forward Control User Manual	608239
Range Rover Workshop Manual 1970-1985 (petrol 3.5)	AKM3630
Range Rover Workshop Manual 1986-1989	SRR660ENWM &
(petrol 3.5 and diesel 2.4 Turbo VM)	LSM180WS4/2
Range Rover Workshop Manual 1990-1994	
(petrol 3.9, 4.2 and diesel 2.5 Turbo VM, 200 Tdi)	LHAWMENA02
Range Rover Workshop Manual 1995-2001 (petrol 4.0, 4.6 and BMW 2.5 diesel)	LRL0326ENGBB
Range Rover Workshop Manual 2002-2005 (BMW petrol 4.4 and BMW 3.0 diesel)	LRL0477
Range Rover Electrical Manual 2002-2005 UK version (petrol 4.4 and 3.0 diesel)	RR02KEMBB
Range Rover Electrical Manual 2002-2005 USA version (BMW petrol 4.4)	RR02AEMBB
Range Rover Parts Catalogue 1970-1985 (petrol 3.5)	RTC9846CH
Range Rover Parts Catalogue 1986-1991 (petrol 3.5, 3.9 and diesel 2.4 and 2.5 Turbo VM)	RTC9908CB
Range Rover Parts Catalogue 1992-1994 MY and 95 MY Classic	
(petrol 3.9, 4.2 and diesel 2.5 Turbo VM, 200 Tdi and 300 Tdi)	RTC9961CB
Range Rover Parts Catalogue 1995-2001 MY (petrol 4.0, 4.6 and BMW 2.5 diesel)	RTC9970CE
Range Rover Owners Handbook 1970-1980 (petrol 3.5)	606917
Range Rover Owners Handbook 1981-1982 (petrol 3.5)	AKM8139
Range Rover Owners Handbook 1983-1985 (petrol 3.5)	LSM0001HB
Range Rover Owners Handbook 1986-1987 (petrol 3.5 and diesel 2.4 Turbo VM)	LSM129HB

Engine Overhaul Manuals for Land Rover and Range Rover

300 Tdi Engine, R380 Manual Gearbox and LT230T Transfer Gearbox Overhaul Manuals	LRL003, 070 & 081
Petrol Engine V8 3.5, 3.9, 4.0, 4.2 and 4.6 Overhaul Manuals	LRL004 & 164
Land Rover/Range Rover Driving Techniques	LR369
Working in the Wild - Manual for Africa	SMR684MI
Winching in Safety - Complete guide to winching Land Rovers and Range Rovers	SMR699MI

Workshop Manual Owners Edition
Land Rover 2 / 2A / 3 Owners Workshop Manual 1959-1983
Land Rover 90, 110 and Defender Workshop Manual Owners Edition 1983-1995
Land Rover Discovery Workshop Manual Owners Edition 1990-1998

All titles available from Amazon or Land Rover specialists
Brooklands Books Ltd., P.O. Box 146, Cobham, Surrey, KT11 1LG, England, UK
Phone: +44 (0) 1932 865051   info@brooklands-books.com   www.brooklands-books.com

www.brooklandsbooks.com

Printed by Printforce, United Kingdom